THE DESIGN CONTINUUM

AN APPROACH TO UNDERSTANDING VISUAL FORMS

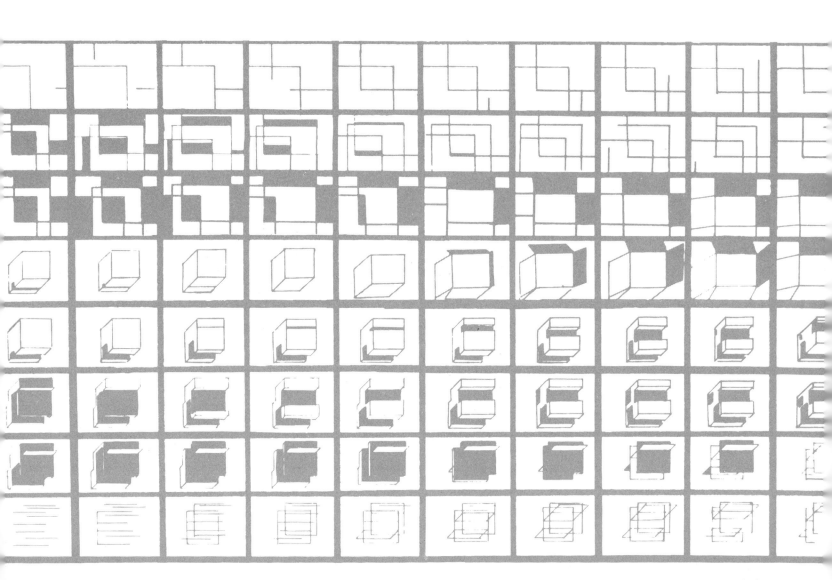

The Design Continuum Concept. In the photograph above we see the entire design continuum illustrated in graphic form. This picture should be scanned back and forth across the page, level by level, from top to bottom: the first level from left to right, then returning from right to left on the next level and continuing such alternation down to the last level. Ideally, this version of the design continuum should be shown by motion picture projection — the design student at Syracuse University who conceived it intended that each individual frame be viewed in rapid sequence for the best effect. If a rendering in the film medium were made, a remarkable illusion of the subtle transition from two-dimensional to three-dimensional space would be clearly demonstrated.

STEWART KRANZ · ROBERT FISHER

THE DESIGN CONTINUUM

AN APPROACH TO UNDERSTANDING VISUAL FORMS

 REINHOLD PUBLISHING CORPORATION/NEW YORK

© 1966, Reinhold Publishing Corporation
All rights reserved
Printed in the United States of America
Library of Congress Card Number 66-14434

Designed by Stewart Kranz and Robert Fisher
Photography by Stewart Kranz, unless otherwise acknowledged
Type set by Lettick Typografic Inc. and Graphic Arts Typographers, Inc.
Printed by The Guinn Company
Color printed in Switzerland by Helvetica Press Incorporated
Bound by Publishers Book Bindery

Contents

Acknowledgements

The authors wish to express their appreciation for the considerable help extended by individuals and organizations in the preparation of this book.

The Environment:
Dr. Frank P. Piskor, Vice-President for Academic Affairs and Dean of Faculties, for creating so favorable a climate for the arts at Syracuse University and for his personal interest in our work; Dr. Laurence Schmeckebier, Dean of the School of Art, Syracuse University, for his genuine interest in our careers and our work in design at the School of Art; the authors' many students in the Syracuse University School of Art, for contributing much hard work to the projects illustrated in this book (a partial list of the participating students will be found on pages 146 and 147).

Creative Participation:
True Fisher and Susan Kranz for their active participation in every phase of producing this book, particularly in their creative ideas relating to the actual concept of the Design Continuum, the choice of visuals to illustrate it, and the logic of the presentation; and, finally, for overseeing the endless details necessary to prepare the photography and the manuscript for publication.

Manuscript Preparation:
Edna Steffen for typing the final manuscript, helping to mail release requests, and for attending to the hundreds of necessary last-minute details; Julia Parr for tirelessly typing our many preliminary drafts; Carol Viney, Secretary, Art Education Department, Syracuse University, for her help with correspondence and other matters.

Bibliographic Research:
Herbert G. Shearer, Ramona Roters, and Monica Zenon, members of the Art Library staff of Syracuse University, for their kind and thoughtful help with this entire project; Fern L. Allen, member of the Architectural Library staff, School of Architecture, Syracuse University, for her many suggestions for our research; Phyllis Donohue for preliminary research for the bibliography; the library staffs at the Metropolitan Museum of Art and the Museum of Modern Art, New York City, for their help with both the photographs and the bibliographic research.

Esthetics:
Robert Greisbaum, Masters Candidate, Advertising Design, and Donald Tompkins, Lecturer, School of Art, Syracuse University, for their perceptive comments; Sigmund

Snyder, Masters Candidate in Sculpture, Syracuse University, for permitting us to use some of his student works for photography.

Photography:
Tony Spinella for his invaluable help in developing our thousands of black-and-white contacts and for his advice on photographic studio problems; Ben Meltzer, with Allen Photo, Syracuse, New York, for his help with the black-and-white negatives and prints; Julius Ersik and Mike Colagero for their work in developing the 4 x 5 color prints; Abby Kinne for sorting and filing our 3500-odd black and white negatives and numbering the contacts; Professor William Demerest, Newhouse Communications Center, School of Journalism, Syracuse University, for his help with photographic problems; Carmen Minella, of the Instructional Communications Department, Syracuse University, for answering our innumerable questions; Leon Rolfe, with Hendricks Photo, Syracuse, New York, for his kind assistance throughout this project; Ben Attas, with Modernage, Inc., New York City, for helping with the preparation and printing, at Modernage, of the black and white photographs.

Publication:
The authors wish to thank the following staff members of the Reinhold Book Division for their energetic assistance: Jean Koefoed, Margaret Holton, Sterling McIlhany, Myron Hall, and Emilio Squeglio. And also Marianna Hassol for her contribution to the editing.

Outside Contributors:

Photographs
The Committee for the Preservation of Abu Simbel, The United Arab Republic Tourist Office, Alexandre Georges, Pedro E. Guerrero, Myron Goldfinger, Joseph E. Seagram and Sons, Inc., Ben Schnall, Ralph Steckler, Herbert Brooks Walker, and the Universal Atlas Cement Division of the United States Steel Corporation.

Architects
Edward Larrabee Barnes, Marcel Breuer, and Philip Johnson.

Art Museums
The authors wish to thank the Museum of Modern Art, the Solomon R. Guggenheim Museum, and The Metropolitan Museum of Art, all in New York City, for permitting the use of reproductions of works from their collections.

Publishers:
The authors are grateful to the following publishers for permission to use quotations from the books listed here; this has greatly enriched their book and will, hopefully, enrich the readers' range of inquiry relative to the Design Continuum.
Addison-Wesley Publishing Company, Inc., Cambridge, Massachusetts: *An Approach to Design*, by Norman Newton; American Federation of Arts, New York: *Design and the Idea*, by Allen Tucker; Bollingen Foundation, New York: *The Art of Sculpture*, by Herbert Read; George Braziller, Inc., New York: *Constantin Brancusi*, by Carola Giedion-Welcker; Farrar, Straus & Giroux, Inc., New York: *Aspects of Form: A Symposium of Form in Nature and Art*, by Lancelot Whyte; Harcourt, Brace & World, Inc., New York: *The New World of Space*, by Le Corbusier; Harvard University Press, Cambridge, Mass.: *An Introduction to the Language of Drawing and Painting*, by Arthur Pope and *Space, Time and Architecture*, by Siegfried Giedon; Mrs. Frances Archipenko, New York: *Archipenko: Fifty Creative Years*, by Alexander Archipenko; Harry Holtzman, Lyme, Conn.: *Plastic Art and Pure Plastic Art*, by Piet Mondrian; Horizon Press, New York: *The Natural House*, by Frank Lloyd Wright; McGraw Hill Book Company, Inc., New York: *Design Fundamentals*, by Robert Scott; The Museum of Modern Art, New York: *Arp*, edited by James Soby from the article "Arp: An Appreciation" by Carola Giedion-Welcker; *The Art of Assemblage*, by William C. Seitz, *Futurism*, by Joshua Taylor, *Medardo Rosso*, by Margaret Scolari Barr, and *The Responsive Eye*, by William C. Seitz; Percy Lund, Humphries and Company, Ltd., London, England: *Henry Moore*, edited by David Sylvester, *An Organic Architecture*, by Frank Lloyd Wright, and *Sculpture: Theme and Variations*, by E. H. Ramsden; Frederick Praeger, Inc., New York: *The Architecture of Fantasy*, by Ulrich Conrads; G. P. Putnam's Sons, New York: *Art as Experience*, by John Dewey and *The New Vision*, by Laszlo Moholy-Nagy; Reinhold Publishing Corporation, New York: *Art in European Architecture*, by Paul Damaz, *Structure and Form*, by Curt Seigel (translated by Thomas Burton), and *Cities* by Lawrence Halprin; Stechert Haefner Publishing Company, New York: *Problem of Form in Painting and Sculpture*, by Adolph Hildebrand. University of California Press, Berkeley and Los Angeles: *Art and Visual Perception*, by Rudolf Arnheim; E. Weyhe, Inc., New York: *Art Forms in Nature*, by Karl Blossfeldt; George Wittenborn, Inc., New York: *The Life of Forms in Art*, second edition, by Henri Focillon and *Contemporary Sculpture, and Evolution in Volume and Space*, by Carola Giedion-Welcker.

"Life is form, and form is the modality of life. The relationships that bind forms together in nature cannot be pure chance, and what we call 'natural life' is in effect a relationship between forms, so inexorable that without it this natural life could not exist. So it is with art as well. The formal relations with a work of art and among different works of art constitute an order for, and a metaphor of, the entire universe." Henri Focillon, Life of Forms in Art, *page 2.*

PART I. THE PREMISE

The Design Continuum

Chaos of Visual Forms in Nature and in the City

Billboards. Cobblestone Streets. A child's balloon. A suspension bridge. All are common forms. Occasionally one will attract and hold our attention for a fleeting moment, but in general the myriad shapes of visual reality pass before us in an incoherent blur. No simple method has been established which would enable us to evaluate these forms with respect to their abstracted similarities or differences. Most of us still see visual reality as a cacophony of separate, dissimilar, and totally unrelated forms.

The museum visitor, for example, who attempts to assimilate and evaluate the works of art contained within even a single gallery is faced with a perplexing dilemma: It is through an understanding of the essential forms of an art object that he can grasp the artist's intent, be it philosophical, spiritual, social, or formal; and yet, without a means of analyzing the abstract qualities of the form, this task can prove quite overwhelming. Assumption is piled upon assumption until the whole vessel settles ignominiously into a sea of frustration. The museum staff often attempts on the most elementary level to help the visitor by organizing its collection into two- and three-dimensional divisions (painting and sculpture) and further subdividing them by period or style. However, because of the tremendous scope of most museum collections, it is difficult if not impossible for museum curators to proceed further with this division.

The separation into two- and three-dimensional works begins to simplify the viewer's task. The logical grouping of all two-dimensional works tells the viewer that, regardless of the content, they are all physically of the same basic form — that is, they are all rendered on a flat surface. Three-dimensional works, which appeal to our tactile, visual, kinesthetic, and (sometimes) acoustical senses, present more difficulties to the observer. Not only do they evoke a response in a greater number of our senses, but they also demand that the viewer comprehend a form that is in a constant state of visual transition and change. In order for the viewer fully to appreciate a three-dimensional work, he must move around it and view it from many different angles. He is essentially experiencing a form in time and space. Thus the problem of perception and consequent understanding of the form is considerably more complex than in two-dimensional works, where his position in relation to the work remains fixed.

1-1 A Photograph of Chaos in Nature.
1-2 A Photograph of Chaos in the City.
(Courtesy of Ralph Steckler.)

Using the approach of art historians, most museums, as indicated previously, organize two- and three-dimensional works chronologically according to period and style. This is without question a valuable way of approaching the study of art forms. However, the need for a comparative method of organization of similar forms that share a common esthetic basis is particularly evident today. The 20th century has been a period of tremendous experimentation in the art world, in which all of the fundamental aspects of visual expression have been profoundly challenged. The exploration of materials, positive and negative space, colors, psychological and subjective content, the time-space continuum, and modes of expression has left a heritage of two- and three-dimensional forms of overwhelming diversity.

One can sympathize with the museum curator's heroic attempts at organizing so disparate a group of art forms. However, the division of works of art solely into two- and three-dimensional categories is not entirely satisfactory, because it offers little assistance to the observer who wants to understand and relate the tremendous variety of forms found within these two divisions. In other fields, such as the natural sciences, this dichotomy is expanded to include more precise and subtle differentiations. The botanist or biologist classifies plant and animal forms according to structural and other physical characteristics. Once these basic differences and similarities are established, the scientist proceeds further with more detailed breakdowns of each plant or animal form. The approach used by scientists has provided a basis for a clear and comprehensive organizational structure of the natural sciences. This process is essentially one of analysis and deduction and seems to point the way toward a more precise categorization of visual form which will be described herein.

Dividing works into two- and three-dimensional forms can provide the initial categories of this organization of visual form. Between the broad concepts of painting and sculpture other form categories, such as textured surfaces and reliefs, may be interjected because they share qualities germane to both art forms. The *textured surface* and *relief* share the frontal aspect of the painting but at the same time physically project outward into the same space that envelops the fully three-dimensional sculptured object. These visual forms are easily identified. Texture may readily be seen in nature, clothing, architectural surfaces, sculpture, and other natural and man-made forms. Similarly, the concept of relief brings to mind Egyptian friezes or, perhaps, the surface of the earth or the moon when viewed or photographed from great altitude.

To most of us the description "three-dimensional" suggests a solid-looking, impenetrable mass. This familiar form might more specifically be called *monolithic mass* and may be defined as an unbroken mass such as the Egyptian pyramids, a grapefruit, a planet, a child's block, a large boulder, the Matterhorn, a dirigible, or an egg. All of these forms share one essential characteristic: They are solid in appearance.

The shell of a broken egg, on the other hand, no longer has the appearance of a solid, impenetrable mass. Instead it is a thin and delicate form that circumscribes space but in no sense fills it or suggests solidity. Since its new nature suggests a plane in three-dimensional form, this kind of form could be called *planar*. Many common objects fall into this category: frying pans, windows, leaves, flower petals, or some of the recent architectural forms made of thin concrete.

The antithesis of monolithic mass may be seen in the analogy of a globe (itself monolithic) upon whose surface are inscribed designations for latitude and longitude. If one were to remove the solid globe and leave only the pattern of intersecting surface lines in space, such a figure could be called a *three-dimensional linear form.* It has no mass, yet it describes a three-dimensional volume. Forms that fall into this designation are surprisingly familiar: the bare branches of trees, a wire litter basket, telephone lines, radio towers, reeds and tall grass, a barbed wire fence, the linear burst of fireworks against the night sky, a spider web, or the skeleton of a fish. To recapitulate, a very rough division of visual forms has been established as follows:

painting and other two-dimensional media
textured surfaces
reliefs
monolithic mass
planar forms
three-dimensional linear forms

Upon deeper investigation one can perceive that these somewhat oversimplified categories omit many areas of visual form. For example, in the area of relief it is possible to subdivide further into *low relief, middle relief,* and *high relief.* Or, in the case of some monolithic forms, the surface may reveal certain projections or concavities like the depression on the top of an apple or the fluting of a Greek column, which, because of the modeling effects of light, begin to break into the solidity of the original mass. Such a form can be defined as a *concave-convex mass.* A further refinement can be derived from much of Henry Moore's sculpture, which is fully penetrated by holes, or from the architecture of the Guggenheim Museum, the massiveness of which is reduced by the flow of space in and around the various component forms of the architecture. Consequently, the new categories of *concave-convex mass* and *fully penetrated mass* can be seen as a logical extension of form from the impenetrable monolith in terms of successive reductions in mass.

A subsequent category that seems to follow the fully penetrated mass is the planar form, which was identified earlier in this discussion. This shell-like form is physically penetrated but differs from the fully penetrated mass by its diminished volume and characteristically thin, plane-like surfaces. Continuing this line of reasoning, a transitional stage can be added between the planar form and the almost totally dissolved mass of the three-dimensional linear form: the *planar-linear form.* Abundant examples of this category exist in nature and in man-made forms: a leaf, a flower with its stem, the surface of a table with its linear legs, a parachute with its planar dome and nylon lines, the human hand with its planar palm and linear fingers, a simple pair of planar eyeglasses with their linear frame. At this point the original categories of visual form have been subdivided and organized as follows:

painting and two-dimensional media	painting and two-dimensional media
textured surfaces	textured surfaces
	low relief
relief	middle relief
	high relief
monolithic mass	monolithic mass
	concave-convex mass
	penetrated mass
planar form	planar form
	planar-linear form
three-dimensional linear form	three-dimensional linear form

This organization is already a long way from the division of form into two-dimensional and three-dimensional groupings, for it is now quite specific as to certain characteristics that allow these forms to be categorized in this manner. But there is a much more subtle, more evasive aspect to this subject which has not been considered although it has been unconsciously applied in determining our various categories. It is the interrelationship of form and space.

Our visual world is one of form and space, mass and void, the tangible and the intangible. We speak of objects as being solid, like an orange; of having texture, like a stone wall; of being linear, as the naked branches of a tree in winter. Yet our description is only partially complete since we have spoken only of the positive form and not of its relationship to the empty environment surrounding it. If objects are considered as combinations of form *and* space, an orange can be interpreted as basically a monolithic impenetrable mass that resists the intrusion of surrounding space. A stone wall can be understood to be essentially a flat surface from which a vast number of small solid forms are pushing outwards into space. Because of their small scale these projections are read as texture. The branches of a tree describe a volume that is composed predominantly of empty space and articulated by a minimum of mass.

It is essential at this point that all the categories of visual forms just outlined be thoroughly analyzed in terms of the relationship between object and environment — or form and space. It will be observed that this organization is as yet incomplete and that additional categories will evolve as logical developments from the present organization.

FLAT TWO-DIMENSIONAL SURFACES

The observer is confronted with a surface that is neutral in its relationship to its environment. It does not physically project into space, nor does the surrounding space penetrate into the surface. It can be conceived of as a completely passive plane that physically connects with space at every point of its surface in exactly the same way. Any sense of depth or feeling of space or form on the two-dimensional surface derives from purely psychological perceptual reasons and is completely illusory in terms of its physical reality.

TEXTURED SURFACES

Strictly speaking, texture may be viewed as the slight upward projection into space of many portions of the surface. The scale of these convexities and concavities is so small in relation to the entire surface, however, that we perceive them as texture rather than as independent units.

LOW RELIEF

In low relief, projections and recessions on the surface begin to dominate the over-all surface texture. Because of the modeling effects of light, either they appear to push gently upward into the spatial environment or, conversely, the environment is permitted to penetrate lightly into the surface. The integrity of the surface is maintained, however, and we perceive all modulations as emanating from or pressing into the surface.

MIDDLE RELIEF

In middle relief, the projections or recessions pull farther away from the surface, or ground plane. They are beginning to assume more importance in relation to the surface from which they emerge. But they are still to be seen as generating from the surface plane or, in other words, as mere continuations or eruptions of the surface into space.

"Taking possession of space is the first gesture of living things, of man and of animals, of plans and of clouds, a fundamental manifestation of equilibrium and of duration. The occupation of space is the first proof of existence. . . .
"Architecture, sculpture and painting are specifically dependent on space, bound to the necessity of controlling space, each by its own appropriate means. The essential thing that will be said here is that the release of esthetic emotion is a special function of space." Le Corbusier, The New World of Space, pages 7 ff.

"Traditionally there was a belief that sculpture begins where material touches space. Thus space was understood as a kind of frame around the mass. We may change the forms of solid volume many times, but the actual existence of the outlines of the forms, beyond which is the beginning of space, seems to be unavoidable." Alexander Archipenko, Archipenko: Fifty Creative Years, page 56.

"A work of art is situated in space. But it will not do to say that it simply exists in space; a work of art treats space according to its own needs, defines space, and even creates such space as may be necessary to it." Henri Focillon, The Life of Forms in Art, page 17.

HIGH RELIEF

One can read high relief as an extreme deformation of a surface. The entire ground plane is in motion, pushing outward into space and permitting space to enter but not to penetrate through the surface.

MONOLITHIC MASS

A monolithic mass is a closed, independent, three-dimensional form that completely rejects the intrusion of the environment, much as our two-dimensional form did in the beginning. It is absolute form, impenetrable, completely surrounded by space (sometimes even floating in space, as a balloon or a dirigible, the opaque skin of which creates the appearance of a solid form), and yet resistant to space. It is form in its most determined state.

CONCAVE-CONVEX MASS

The arrogance of pure form is tempered slightly by the admission of some of the environmental space into the form — but only some. Determined to remain basically solid, the monolith, like the low relief, is modified by means of concavities and convexities. But similarly, the integrity of the basic form is preserved.

PENETRATED MASS

Slowly the monolithic mass begins to relent, and space is allowed to penetrate the solid through deep depressions and holes. There is still a sense of three-dimensional mass, but space is beginning to assume a much more active role.

PLANAR FORMS

Though the total form is still completely three-dimensional in character, it has deteriorated into a series of planes that take on the role of space articulators. These planes serve to divide and mold space much as an architect considers the walls of his rooms; they are vital but subordinate to the total shape of the space within. Thus the balance of form and space is now tipped in favor of space.

PLANAR-LINEAR FORM

Further dissolution of mass is evident here. This concept may be illustrated with the example of a waterfall. As a sheet of running water flows out and down into unconfined space, it maintains for a moment its planar quality. But soon the forces of gravity overcome this coherent surface and a transformation occurs as the plane begins to splay into a series of controlled and rather stout linear appendages. Such a form is short-lived, however, for gravity again fractures this transient stage and the water breaks into thousands of individual linear streams before it crashes into a mist. Such a phenomenon can be termed a planar-linear form; it is an interplay of lines and planes.

THREE-DIMENSIONAL LINEAR FORM

In this final phase of three-dimensional form, space dominates form. It has won its unrelenting battle with solid monolithic mass, for all that remains of positive form is the barest of linear elements. These elements play a most significant role, however, for without them space has neither articulation nor form: they serve to structure space in the purest sense. Ironically, even in the most triumphant state, space still depends upon positive form for its ultimate articulation.

In evaluating the visual terms of the foregoing categories, the interaction of form and space is clearly evident. Up to and including the monolithic state, form has been the aggressor with respect to a relatively passive space. It has pushed its way outward into space, all the while maintaining its integrity as form. Having reached its most positive statement as a monolith, the mass succumbed to the unrelenting pressure of the surrounding negative environment. Space has now become the aggressor. It pushes and probes into the solid mass until it breaks through completely. It dissolves the mass even further into planes and finally into lines. Its ultimate victory is the line in space, in which state an otherwise shapeless space is given form by an absolute minimum of mass.

Up to this point a smooth development of form occurs from a two-dimensional surface through high relief, and an equally smooth and logical transition is apparent from monolithic mass to a three-dimensional linear composition. But what about the obvious breach between high relief and monolithic form? This is the most complex phase in the evolution of form, and it is an area for which unlimited examples may be found in nature and in architecture, sculpture, and other man-made objects. Therefore it is important that the concept of emerging form in its development from high relief to monolithic mass be clarified.

The visual condition of high relief was defined earlier as an extreme deformation of a surface. But it is still a surface which is under consideration. In a high relief, though large portions of this ground plane are thrusting upward or are being depressed, these portions still belong to the surface. But what would happen if some of the upward-thrusting portions of the surface started to assume a more independent three-dimensional character? For the purposes of this discussion, these emerging projections will be defined as *ground forms* that exist in conjunction with a surrounding physical environment: the ground plane. An analogy can be drawn with the relationship between the pregnant mother and the developing fetus. In one sense the fetus is totally dependent on the mother for life, yet it exists independently of her within the womb environment, joined to her only by the placenta. Another clear analogy would be an aerial view of rolling hill country dotted with farm buildings and the roving forms of cattle in the pastures. In such a composition the predominant feature is the undulating environment of the hillside. Subordinate to this environment are the many small but independent ground forms — in this case the farm buildings and the cattle. The total composition of relief and ground forms can be called an *environmental relief*.

A further development of this premise leads to a concentration on the role of the ground form as it becomes the dominant element in a receding and progressively subordinate environment. In the environmental relief the ground forms are simply secondary elements. Now, however, they begin to assume a more active role in the total composition of form and environment. Such strong emerging forms can be called *environmental sculpture*. These forms and their surrounding environment have obtained approximately equal status. One can get a feeling for this type of visual statement by looking at the skyline of an oil field. The towering derricks, as environmental sculpture, sharply project into space, punctuating the total composition with their vertical relationship to the plain on which they stand.

The evolution of form has progressed from a condition of simple relief to one of relief and subordinate ground forms, and then to a condition where the ground form or the environmental sculpture is as visually significant as the surrounding relief. Now a third and final phase might be anticipated in the transition between relief and monolithic form: the *sculpture with base*. In this last category emphasis is placed on the emerging sculptural form, whereas the physical environment assumes a completely subordinate role. In a sense we might say that the environment has suffered a complete inversion of the emphasis that it formerly enjoyed in the environmental relief state. At this point

". . . it is in the nature of any organic building to grow from its site, come out of the ground into the light — the ground itself held always as a component basic part of the building itself. And then we have primarily the new ideal of building as organic. A building dignified as a tree in the midst of nature." Frank Lloyd Wright, The Natural House, *page 50.*

it exists as a mere appendage to the imposing and triumphant sculptural form. One finds numerous examples of this form in the fine arts such as Boccioni's *Bottle in Space,* Rodin's series of hands (*Hand of God, Hand of the Devil,* etc.), and Medardo Rosso's sculpted figures.

It would serve the purposes of this discussion to clarify the significance and function of the base. The base is often treated as the transitional element between the supporting plane (floor, wall, ceiling, ground) and the form. In some instances the base will serve a vital functional role as a stabilizing element that emphasizes its structural relationship to the sculptural form itself. In other cases, such as in most of the work of Brancusi, the base will serve a predominately esthetic function, merging visually with the sculptural form. In either case the base performs an important part in the impression of the total work and cannot be dismissed as an extraneous element.

It can be noted that progressively less emphasis has been placed on the physical environment for emerging forms, and increasing emphasis has been placed on the character of the emerging sculpture. The next logical step is the monolith, wherein the last vestiges of a base are discarded and the solid three-dimensional form emerges as a total and self-defining entity.

This discussion has presented a logical sequential organization, or *continuum,* of visual form. Its purpose is to aid the observer in understanding and relating the multitudinous variety of natural and manmade forms. Through objective analysis, the following categories have been established and ordered into *a Design Continuum:*

painting and two-dimensional media
textured surface
low relief
middle relief
high relief
environmental relief
environmental sculpture
sculpture with base
monolithic mass
concave-convex mass
penetrated mass
planar form
planar-linear form
three-dimensional linear form

The Design Continuum deals with the realm of visual experience, and consequently, though it is possible to describe them verbally, these categories of form are seen most clearly through a sequential, visual presentation of logically related forms. Initially three different series — wood, kitchen utensils, and classical sculpture — are photographically presented in order to illustrate this concept.

Nature: Wood Series

On the following five pages the Design Continuum is visualized by using a common organic form: wood in its natural state. Here are forms with which we are all familiar: tree branches, root systems, fallen logs, twigs, end-grain patterns, bark, and old tree stumps. Perhaps we will now look at these myriad forms in a new way, a way that might enable us better to understand and interrelate their complex diversity.

1-3 Two-dimensional Linear Composition.   **1-4** Two-dimensional Textural Composition.   **1-5** Textural Relief.

Nature: Wood Series *(Figures 1-3 through 1-17)*

1-6 Low Relief.　　　　　**1-7** Middle Relief.　　　　　**1-8** High Relief.

1-9 Environmental Relief.

1-10 Environmental Sculpture.

1-11 Sculpture with Dominating Base.

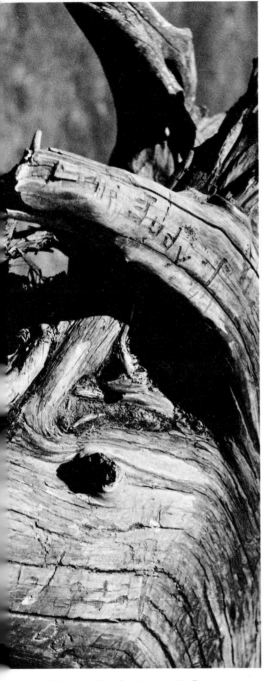

1-12 Dominating Sculpture with Base.

1-13 Monolithic Mass.

1-14 Concave-Convex Mass.

1-15 Penetrated Mass.

1-16 Highly Penetrated Mass.

1-17 Three-dimensional Linear Form.

Man-Made Objects: Kitchen Utensils Series

An egg beater, a bread basket, a cookie mold, a Charlie McCarthy teaspoon, and a funnel — we have lived with these objects all our lives. Most of us pay little attention to the form of everyday objects, yet this pictorial series reveals the rich diversity of form inherent in such mundane items. This second illustration of the Design Continuum is ordered in much the same manner as the initial wood series. For the purposes of this evaluation, the utilitarian aspects of these objects should be completely ignored; it is only their outward form which is under consideration.

1—18

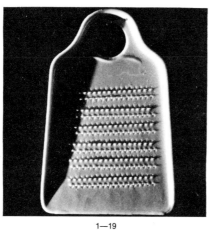

1—19

1—20

1—21

Man-Made Objects: Kitchen Utensils
(Figures 1-18 through 1-33)
1-18 Two-dimensional Linear Composition.
1-19 Textural Composition.
1-20 Very Low Relief.
1-21 Color Relief.
1-22 Middle Relief.
1-23 High Relief.
1-24.Environmental Relief.
1-25 Sculpture with Base: Balanced Emphasis.
1-26 Sculpture with Base: Sculptural Form Dominates.
1-27 Monolithic Mass.
1-28 Concave-Convex Mass.
1-29 Planar Form with Slight Penetration.
1-30 Penetrated Planar Form.
1-31 Open Planar Form.
1-32 Planar-Linear Form.
1-33 Three-dimensional Linear Form.

1—27

1—28

1—26

1—29

1—22

1—23

1—24

1—25

1—30

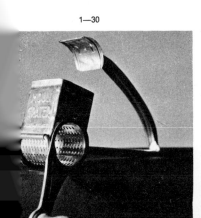

1—31

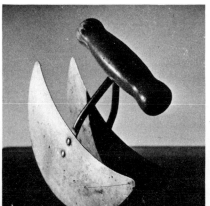

1—32

1—33

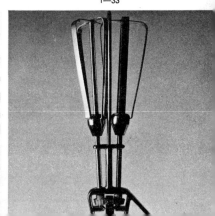

Classical Sculpture Series *(Figures 1-34 through 1-43)*

Both in an organic material like wood and in the indigenous utensils of man, we find a condition in which visual forms have been created primarily out of functional necessity rather than out of any specific system of esthetics. If we turn now to the art world and particularly to classic art forms, we find quite a contrary *raison d'etre.* Bound by an esthetic order that governed the form in which reality, ideology, and mythology were represented, the ancient Egyptians, Etruscans, Greeks, and Romans created sculpture that was the conceptual antithesis of the functional esthetic seen in the wood or the kitchen utensils. Yet even though this dichotomy exists, it has little bearing on a purely objective view of these classic sculptural forms, for they are, after all, simply forms.

1-34 Two-dimensional Linear Composition: Etruscan Antiquities, mirror, engraved design, *Peleus Surprising Thetis* (names are inscribed). (The Metropolitan Museum of Art, Rogers Fund, 1909.)

1-35 Low Relief: Egyptian Sculpture, XIX Dynasty (Reign of Rameses I - Seti I), from the Temple of Rameses I at Abydos, *The King and Queen Make Offerings to Osiris* (Queen Sitra and King Rameses I make offerings to Osiris, Isis, and Hathor). (The Metropolitan Museum of Art, Gift of J. Pierpont Monrgan, 1911.)

1-36 Middle Relief: Roman Sculpture from Tarentum *Kerakles Carrying the Erymathian Boar on his Shoulder*, (marble). (The Metropolitan Museum of Art, Rogers Fund, 1913.)

1-37 High Relief and Emerging Ground Forms: Cast Reproduction of Roman Sculpture, Augustan period, 1st Century B.C. - 1st Century A.D. (original in the Museo Nazionale, Ravenna). Augustus, Livia, and perhaps Agrippa and Marcellus (marble). (The Metropolitan Museum of Art.)

1-38 Environmental Sculpture: Egyptian Sculpture from Gizeh (ca. 2420 B.C.) *The Steward Memy-Sabu and his Wife* (white limestone, originally painted, about 62 centimeters high). (The Metropolitan Museum of Art, Rogers Fund, 1948.)

1-39 Monolithic Mass: Cypriote Sculpture (7th Century B.C.) *Statue of a Bearded Votary Wearing Helmet and Assyrian Dress* (more than life-size, limestone). (The Metropolitan Museum of Art, The Cesnola Collection, Purchased by subscription, 1874-1876.)

1-40 Concave-Convex Mass with Slight Penetration: Greek Sculpture (615 - 600 B.C.), Statue of a Youth of the *Apollo* Type (marble). (The Metropolitan Museum of Art, Fletcher Fund, 1932.)

1-41 Fully Penetrated Mass: Roman Copy of a Greek Work (440 - 430 B.C.), *Wounded Amazon* (pentelic marble). Original attributed to Polykleitos or Kresilas. (The Metropolitan Museum of Art, Gift of John D. Rockefeller, Jr., 1932.)

1—37

1—38

1—39

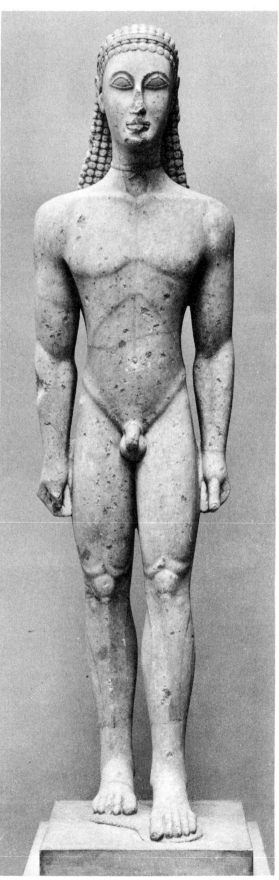

1—40

1—41

1-42 Open Spatial Composition: Cast Reproduction of Greek Sculpture (Late 2nd or Early 1st Century B.C.), *The Borghese Warrior* (inscribed with the name of the sculptor Agasias; original found at Antium and now in the Louvre, Paris). (The Metropolitan Museum of Art, The Cullum Collection, 1895.)

1-43 Planar-Linear Form: Etruscan Sculpture (7th to 5th Century B.C.), *Fighting Warrior* (Ares?). (The Metropolitan Museum of Art, Purchased by subscription, 1896.)

1—42

1—43

Photographic Methods of Presentation

In order to graphically present in as clear a manner as possible the various form categories side by side in a series, it is necessary to shift the camera angle to capture the best position for viewing a particular work. For example, flat two-dimensional work, textured surfaces, and reliefs are most clearly viewed in a straight-on photograph in which the lens of the camera is roughly parallel to the frontal plane of the work. In examples of forms emerging from a relief it is essential to capture the feeling of the projection of these forms from the surface. Three-dimensional objects, on the other hand, are shown most advantageously from a three-quarter view or from full side views.

Comparative Series of Student Work
(Figures 1-44 through 1-59)

The student project presented on the following two pages is photographed from two views — straight above and at oblique angles — and both views are shown simultaneously. This will give the reader a clearer idea of what is happening to visual form as it alters in appearance and character and should establish a frame of reference for later series. Future series will be treated in a slightly different manner by combining the two views in one series. Therefore up to and including high relief, the works are shown approximately straight on. The next few classifications of visual form — environmental relief, environmental sculpture, and sculpture with base — are photographed at increasingly lower angles until monolithic form is reached. From that point on, the subject matter is photographed from a side view only.

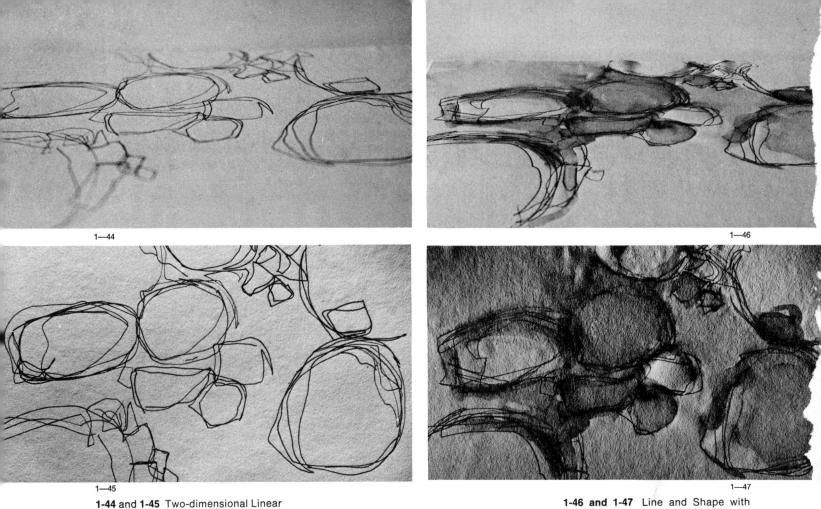

1—44

1—46

1—45

1—47

1-44 and **1-45** Two-dimensional Linear
Composition.

1-46 and 1-47 Line and Shape with
Suggestion of Texture.

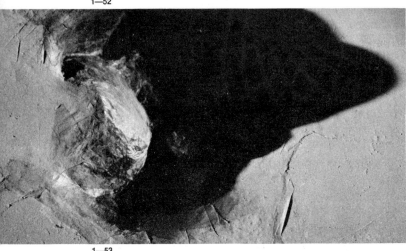

1—52

1—54

1—53

1—55

1-52 and **1-53** Essentially Monolithic
Three-dimensional Mass.

1-54 and **1-55** Penetrated Three-
dimensional Mass with Concavities
and Convexities.

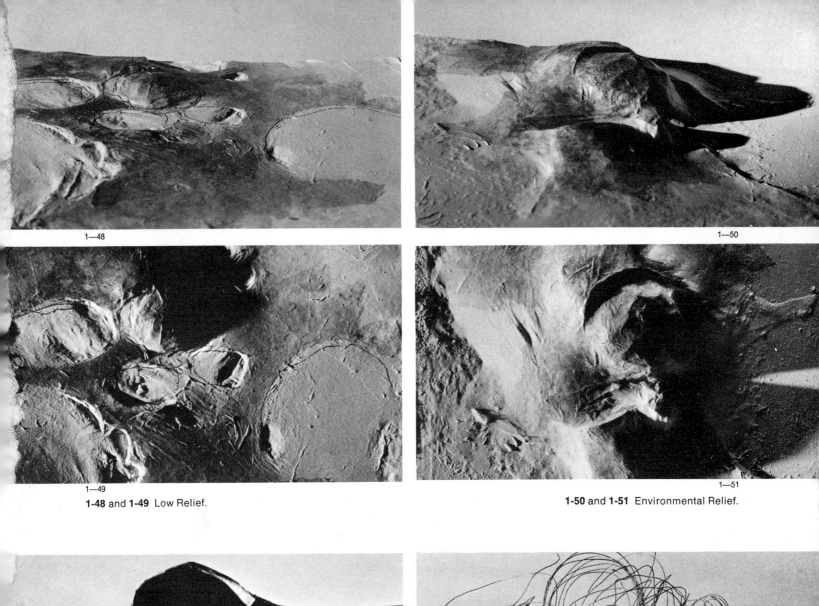

1-48 and 1-49 Low Relief.

1-50 and 1-51 Environmental Relief.

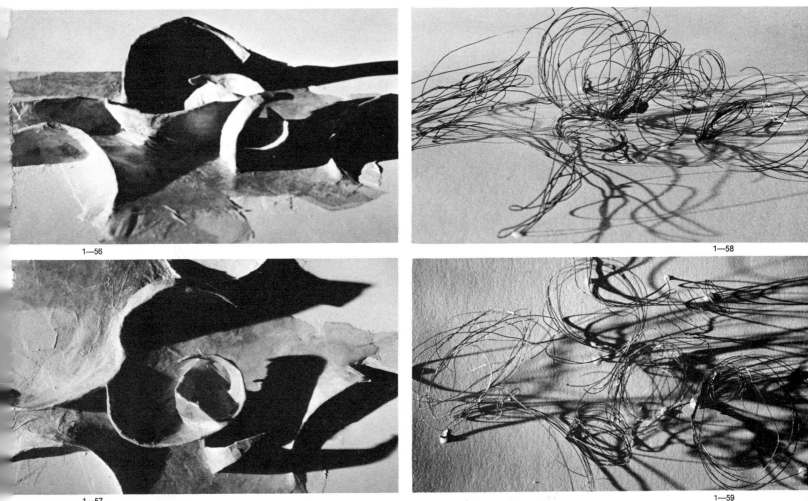

1-56 and 1-57 Dissolution of Three-dimensional Form into Planes.

1-58 and 1-59 Final Dissolution of Form into a Three-dimensional Linear Composition.

Scale and Frame of Reference

As the reader may have noted in the preceding series of comparative photographs, the vantage point of the observer must be kept constantly in mind when attempting to appreciate and analyze two- and three-dimensional forms. Quite often man forgets his unique posture in relationship to the animal world; as a biped, he stands vertical in relationship to the horizontal plane of the earth, whereas the animal world, being quadruped, accepts a horizontal frame of reference with apparent equanimity. We can only speculate on the extent to which man's ability to stand vertically on two feet has influenced his entire esthetic point of view. Modern technology has enabled man to alter his viewing position radically, and consequently he must be prepared to accept an ever-increasing, perhaps even alarming, change in his normal frame of reference. We do not hesitate to accept a long, slow descent from the sky by helicopter; nor do we question the view of the earth obtained from a skyscraper or from a satellite orbiting 150 miles above its surface. Even close-up camera and television views of distant planets are becoming rather commonplace. On the other end of visual perception, the revolution in frame of reference is equally astounding. The microphotograph and other sophisticated means of recording the structure of the most minute forms of matter again seem, for all their ethereal beauty, quite usual.

A modern classic, *The New Landscape,* by Gyorgy Kepes, professor of visual design at the Massachusetts Institute of Technology, deals with precisely these concepts. Today, Kepes points out, the world of science and optics has extended man's vision immeasurably. He illustrates this new landscape of vision in such a way as to create a feeling for the visual relationships between science and art. Rather than reacting to the scientific field with fearful withdrawal, Kepes contends that the artist should begin to assess the extraordinary visual creations of science as the source of new directions. Professor Kepes cites three groupings of scientific instruments that bring new orders of visual magnitude to the human eye: the telescope and the microscope, for tremendous magnification; the X-ray, infrared and ultraviolet rays for simultaneous interior and exterior viewing; the still camera time exposure and stroboscopic lighting methods as well as other sophisticated photographic techniques for visual extensions.

Another valuable contribution to this field is the work of Professor William Harlow, of the State University College of Forestry, Syracuse University. Professor Harlow has gained broad recognition for his experiments in the field of time lapse photography. His methods enable the observer to experience, through the use of the motion picture medium, the development of a form over a prolonged period of time. In some ways his work is a logical extension of the attempts of the Italian Futurists to show the object in time as well as in space.

Newhouse Center and Crouse College Series
(Figures 1-60 through 1-89)

The reader should now direct his attention to the next series of comparative photographs (pages 36 through 41). He will find a grouping of paired photographs on a contemporary building, the Samuel I. Newhouse Communications Center, designed by I. M. Pei, and a late 19th-century building, the H. B. Crouse College, both situated on the Syracuse University campus in Syracuse, New York. Camera lenses of varying degrees of magnification were used to produce this comparative series. The range of extension went from that of a normal 50-millimeter lens to the magnification of a 450-millimeter telephoto lens.

It should be noted that the human eye has a magnification power similar to that of a 50-millimeter lens on a 35-millimeter camera. We accept quite readily the magnification of human vision through the medium of the camera. To emphasize that what we see is a direct function of our proximity to the object in the path of our vision the observer's frame of reference is deliberately shifted in these next photographs. By simply switching the lens on the camera the viewer can instantly be transported from a distant view of the Newhouse Center to an extreme close-up of a marble bench in the interior of the building. Through the eye of the camera the reader can experience a building in time and space with relative ease. It is hoped that the reader, when viewing the objects on his own, will eventually sever his dependence on the selectivity of the camera and begin automatically to shift his frame of reference. When he has achieved this the observer will be able to accept the most complex combination of visual forms — such as are to be observed in a building like Crouse College — and finally be able to organize them into a comprehensible whole.

1—60 (above)   1—61 (below)   1—62 (above)   1—63 (below)   1—64 (above)   1—65 (below)

1-60 Two-dimensional Linear Composition: The mullions dividing the modular window area, which provides illumination for the interior court of Newhouse Communications Center, create a two-dimensional linear pattern when seen from this particular vantage point.

1-61 Two-dimensional Linear Composition: Here the mullions dividing the colored glass panes in this Neo-Gothic window in Crouse College again create a flat pattern of lines which is accentuated by the intense exterior illumination.

1-62 Textural Composition: In this close-up view of the highly polished surface of the marble bench in the interior court of Newhouse Center a subtle textural grain is revealed. At the same time the high reflectivity of the marble surface echoes the modular character of the overhead source (figure 1-60).

1-63 Textural Composition: In this exterior close-up view of a wall surface of Crouse College the fine texture of the stone is enhanced by the delicate filigree of ivy.

1-64 Very Low Relief: Whenever we use the human eye as a receptor, the distance between the viewer and the subject area determines the appearance of that area. Notice in this particular example that the stairs, which logic tells us are fully three-dimensional, appear to be an area of very low relief because of our viewing angle and the particular distance from subject to object.

1-65 Very Low Relief: In this case, the south façade of Crouse College, the viewer's distance from the subject is sufficient to make architectural details of actual physical prominence blend into a pattern of very low relief.

1—66 (above)   1—67 (below)   1—68 (above)   1—69 (below)   1—70 (above)   1—71 (below)

1-66 Low Relief: In this case, the distance from subject to viewer has decreased and consequently the relief appears to be more pronounced. It should also be noted that in the last comparative series (figure 1-64) the angle of vision of the viewer prevented a full perception of the three-dimensional character of the staircase. Here the viewer is above the subject, so that he can see both horizontal and vertical planes.

1-67 Low Relief: The relief of the windows located above the south entrance of Crouse College appears to be slightly higher than the windows in figure 1-65 because of greater proximity of viewer to subject area.

1-68 Middle Relief: The viewer has at this point drawn closer to the subject area, and as a result this small architectural detail on the Newhouse south façade reads as a middle relief.

1-69 Middle Relief: Here, as in the figure above (figure 1-68), the viewer is very close to the subject area. Hence the relief on this south door is quite prominent.

1-70 High Relief: In this instance, the relief is seen as part of a major architectural member (a lintel) as well as an embellishment of a two-dimensional surface. It should be noted that the sense of relief is heightened even more because of this relationship.

1-71 High Relief: Like the figure above (figure 1-70), this strong relief embellishment is also part of a dominant architectural member (a post).

1—72 (above)　　1—73 (below)　　　　　　　1—74 (above)　　1—75 (below)

1-72 Environmental Relief: One can consider the floor area of this interior court of Newhouse Communications Center as an environment from which the stairs, bench, and balustrade emerge as individual three-dimensional ground forms. It should be noted that the flat surfaces of the bench and stair areas derive their essential character from the flat two-dimensional character of the floor plane.

1-73 As in the illustration above (figure 1-72), the balustrade functions in relationship to the environment as a three-dimensional ground form. In contrast to the rather severe character of the Newhouse court, the soft curves of the Crouse College balustrade reflect the fluid and organic nature of the relief

embellishment on the wall plane.

1-74 Environmental Sculpture: As the viewer's distance from the building is significantly increased, he may then consider the entire Newhouse Center as a bold sculpture in a sympathetic horizontal environment.

1-75 Environmental Sculpture: Here again, as in the figure above (figure 1-74), the viewing distance has been increased. The steeply inclined roof surfaces of Crouse College serve as an appropriate environment for the small decorative turrets and the massive verticals of the north belfry tower. Both tower and turrets may be defined as sculpture that emulates the essential character of its environment.

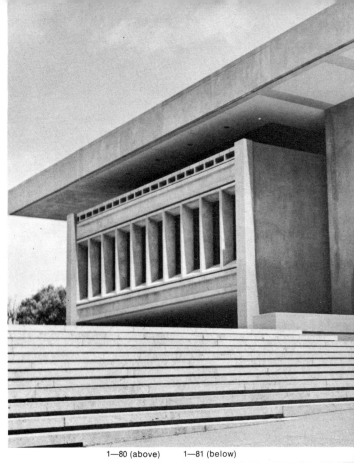

1—76 (above)   1—77 (below)   1—78 (above)   1—79 (below)   1—80 (above)   1—81 (below)

1-76 Sculpture with Base: In this comparative series (figures 1-76, 1-77) the viewer is very close to the subject, because a small architectural detail is under consideration. In the balustrade at Newhouse Center we sense a distinct separation between the solid base of the balustrade and the conjoined but independent sculpture of the railing.

1-77 Sculpture with Base: The closed turret of Crouse College functions as a sculpture that rises from an applied column serving as its base.

1-78 Monolithic Mass: The view of this southwest corner of Newhouse Center is particularly monolithic in character. The ponderous mass of the concrete forms staunchly resists the intrusion of the surrounding space.

1-79 Monolithic Mass: This turret on the southwest corner of Crouse College has the same monolithic quality that we observe in the Newhouse example above (figure 1-78).

1-80 Penetrated Mass: The west façade of Newhouse Center, seen from this vantage point, reveals a significant intrusion of exterior space into the building's mass.

1-81 Penetrated Mass: The jagged contours of Crouse College suggest a mass that dynamically interacts with the surrounding space. The belfry, roofs, and turrets now project upward in such a manner as to permit the intrusion of space in the broad expanses between their solid mass.

39

1—82 (above)   1—83 (below)   1—84 (above)   1—85 (below)

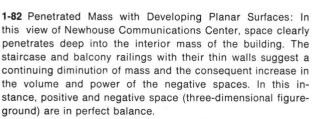

1-82 Penetrated Mass with Developing Planar Surfaces: In this view of Newhouse Communications Center, space clearly penetrates deep into the interior mass of the building. The staircase and balcony railings with their thin walls suggest a continuing diminution of mass and the consequent increase in the volume and power of the negative spaces. In this instance, positive and negative space (three-dimensional figure-ground) are in perfect balance.

1-83 Penetrated Mass with Developing Planar Surfaces: This southeast portico of Crouse College also reveals a deep

penetration of exterior space into the building's mass.

1-84 Deeply Penetrated Planar Form: This descending staircase in Newhouse Center illustrates a deeply penetrated planar form. The powerful negative volume of the stairwell dominates the thin planes of the staircase, which literally seems to float in space.

1-85 Deeply Penetrated Planar Form: The same interaction of thin planar forms we observed above (figure 1-84) occurs in this Crouse College staircase. In addition, the wooden railings suggest the beginnings of linear three-dimensional forms.

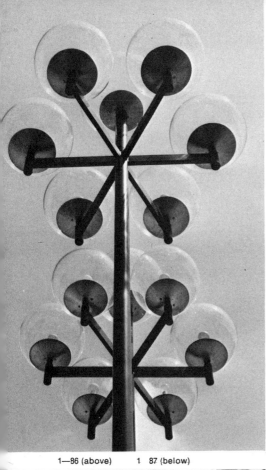

1—86 (above)   1 87 (below)   1—88 (above)   1—89 (below)

1-86 Planar-Linear Form: The planar elements of this composition are illustrated by the transparent glass globes and their supporting saucer-shaped fittings. The thin lamp column with its radiating stems serves to illustrate linear elements.

1-87 Planar-Linear Form: The shingled roof surfaces below the open turret illustrate the planar aspects of this composition. The thin, embellished columns trace a three-dimensional linear pattern against the sky.

1-88 Three dimensional Linear Form: This overhead skylight in Newhouse Center provides the viewer with an excellent ex-ample of a three-dimensional linear composition. Because of the intense illumination, the planar surfaces of the mullions and window panes visually disintegrate so that the dominant emphasis is that of lines in space.

1-89 Three-dimensional Linear Form: In this Crouse College skylight, the visual phenomenon that we noticed in the example above (figure 1-88) is repeated. It should be noted that this last example represents the final dissolution of three-dimensional mass into lines in space.

41

Toward a New Understanding of Visual Forms

The *Design Continuum* concept exists most clearly as a visual expression. It attempts to organize as objectively as possible the things we see. It should be pointed out that this is clearly only one of the many ways to study visual form. The methods of art history, of science, or of those who would group forms of the same media, function, structure, and so forth, should hardly be discounted. All these other approaches are of equal validity and all serve a needed function in clarifying visual phenomena.

One of the most important features of this method of analysis is its iconoclasm, in the sense that objects are grouped from a purely objective visual form standpoint, independent of their function, their emotional appeal, their medium, or their historical significance. Without hesitation, nature has been compared to man-made objects, architecture and sculpture to utilitarian things, eggs to pyramids, and telephone wires to trees. Man's creations are thus related to those of nature because only the most superficial aspect of each object — its form — has been considered. This act of oversimplification does not necessarily make the approach superficial, however, since the intention of this organization is only to take a first organizing step with an idea that may help to create a firmer basis for deeper and more penetrating analysis of two- and three-dimensional forms. Without this first step we are as helpless as the museum visitor or the man in the street trying to grasp the complexities of the visual forms assumed by reality.

The authors hope to loosen the sometimes restraining bonds of art history and of even that sacred word, "function," and just let the observer relax and absorb the purely visual aspects of his environment. In the process the reader must be able to accept sudden changes in scale due to a shift in his frame of reference; he must begin to realize that what we perceive as a given form is completely dependent upon our relation to it and to other forms. The viewer should look first and ask questions later; he should not always insist that he know what the object is, and his preconceptions must no longer remain the basis for his understanding of what he sees. Hopefully it will not be too much or

"Form has a meaning — but it is a meaning entirely its own, a personal and specific value that must not be confused with the attributes we impose upon it. . . . An architectural mass, a relationship of tones, a painter's touch, an engraved line, exist and possess value, primarily in and of themselves." Henri Focillon, The Life of Forms in Art, *pages 3 ff.*

too upsetting to ask him to accept eggs and water towers, waffles and building façades, sea shells and cityscapes, as being of related visual form.

A further result of approaching visual form in this manner is the abandonment of the insistence that art is a thing separate from life or that it consists of objects that one must isolate in a museum. Clearly, form exists in all things, humble or majestic. The relative beauty or artistic value of each object is up to the observer to decide. Even further, it is necessary to eliminate the senseless separations existing within the art field: Painting, sculpture, and architecture remain isolated from one another, and crafts and industrial design are separated from the "art world" because of their functional aspects or techniques. Our visual environment is infinitely richer when we destroy the artificial boundaries established by preconceptions or self-interest. The value to the artist of this interpretative freedom is obvious. He, of all people, should be open to stimuli from every conceivable direction. Yet how ironic it is that so many people in this field are not only ignorant of the visual excitement in other areas but adamant in maintaining their self-imposed isolation.

To the layman, a basic understanding of visual form, without the usual dates, periods, style names, or even knowledge of function, can be the first important step toward a far richer visual life. If the average person can learn to appreciate the qualities of form in the most mundane objects — a drinking glass, a toaster, a mixing spoon, a chair, or a teapot — so much more can be added to his enjoyment of them. Too often the layman is frightened by the idea that before he can learn to see he must know the esthetic history, social ingredients, and psychological implications of the object of his attention. "What is it?" "What does it do?" "Why did the artist do it like this?" "How am I supposed to react to this work?" "Who created it?" All these questions fill the minds of the typical observer of art forms in a museum. They block his immediate and spontaneous reaction to the work. They establish a barrier to essential understanding. They leave him in doubt, alienated, antagonistic, a victim of conventional attitudes. Yet this same person will, without thinking, react to nature's landscape, become excited by Times Square at night, hang a particular painting in his home just because he likes it. If there is nothing pretentious about his relationship to visual form in these experiences, why then must there be so much hesitation in his reaction to what is formally designated as "art"?

All the paraphernalia and mysticism with which the art world has surrounded itself have served only to sever its relation to the ordinary experiences of man. And the more alienated the layman becomes, the more the art world withdraws into its own esoteric terminology, its fads and shock tactics, its closed dilettante society. How tragic is the loss of esthetic appreciation in a world of such infinite visual form and beauty. Yet until one begins to gain a sense of order by recognizing the similarities and disparities of form in all things, his visual environment will remain a tangled maze of seemingly unrelated objects which precludes its understanding. The authors hope, in the presentation and clarification of the Design Continuum, to challenge this chaos.

As the reader progresses through the various series, their growing complexity should be pointed out. Whereas the initial series relate only to themselves, the series in Part Two of this book are comparative and show similar forms existing in nature and in architecture. Part Three goes even further, and in Part Four, the color section, nature, various common man-made objects, and student design projects are simultaneously related.

1—90

1—91

1—92

1—93

Mexican Folk Art Series *(Figures 1-90 through 1-105).* One has little trouble understanding or appreciating these works of Mexican folk art. Somehow the primitiveness of their genesis makes them less imposing. Yet, in these unpretentious examples lies a diversity of form as rich and varied as in the most conceptually complex esthetic forms. By isolating certain qualities of form inherent in the objects, a simple craft can be related to a more highly developed art form.

1-90 Two-dimensional Linear Composition.
1-91 Two-dimensional Composition of Shapes.
1-92 Texture.
1-93 Very Low Relief.
1-94 Low Relief.
1-95 Middle Relief.
1-96 High Relief.
1-97 Environmental Relief.
1-98 Environmental Sculpture.
1-99 Sculpture with Base.
1-100 Monolithic Mass.
1-101 Concave-Convex Mass.
1-102 Penetrated Mass.
1-103 Highly Penetrated Mass.
1-104 Planar-Linear Form.
1-105 Three-dimensional Form.

1—99

1—101

1—100

1—98

1—94

1—95

1—96

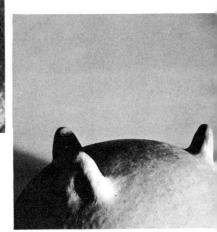

1—97

1—105

1—103

1—102

1—104

45

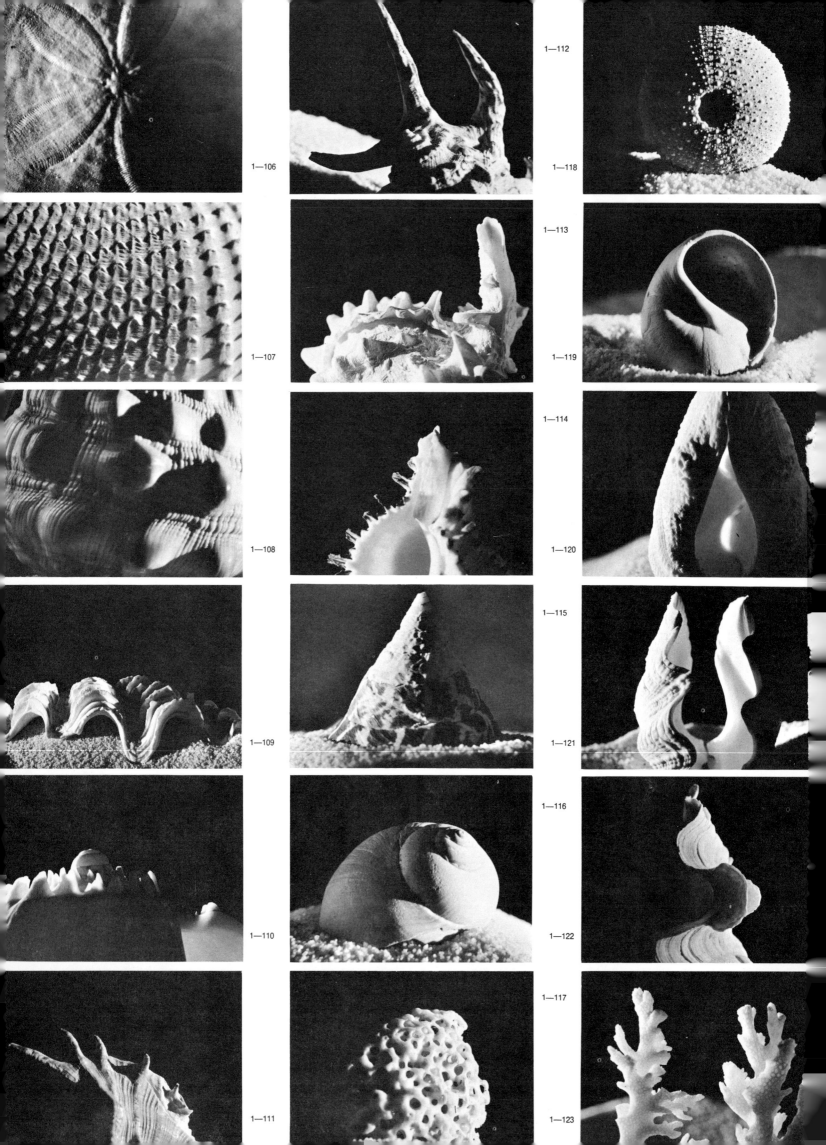

1—106

1—107

1—108

1—109

1—110

1—111

1—112

1—113

1—114

1—115

1—116

1—117

1—118

1—119

1—120

1—121

1—122

1—123

Shell Series *(Figures 1-106 through 1-123).* By ordering these sea-shells along the lines of the Design Continuum they assume a kinship with other natural and man-made forms. Our response of delight in the shells is simple and unaffected even though the range of forms to be found is incredibly diverse.

1-106 Two-dimensional Linear Composition.
1-107 Texture.
1-108 Middle Relief.
1-109 High Relief.
1-110 Environmental Relief with Slightly Emerging Form.
1-111 Environmental Relief with More Pronounced Emerging Forms.
1-112 Environmental Sculpture.
1-113 Sculpture with Base: Dominant Emerging Form.
1-114 Sculpture with Slight Suggestion of Base.
1-115 Monolithic Mass.
1-116 Concave-Convex Mass.
1-117 Slightly Penetrated Mass.
1-118 Penetrated Mass.
1-119 Penetrated Mass with Developing Planar Surfaces.
1-120 Closed Planar Form.
1-121 Open Planar Form.
1-122 Planar-Linear Form.
1-123 Three-dimensional Linear Form.

Modern Sculpture Series

For the last group of illustrations in Part One a series of forms has been reserved which are perhaps the most widely discussed and seemingly the most difficult to understand — even, at times, for the most sophisticated observers. Contemporary sculpture, with its extreme diversity of premise and form of expression, often confounds the observer as a direct consequence of these very strengths. Yet if one looks closely at the thousands of works created by sculptors today, he can begin to organize these multifarious forms into categories of sculptural expression along the lines of the Design Continuum; in other words, some works are predominantly two-dimensional, some reliefs, sculpture with base, monolithic, planar, and so forth. Once some kind of order in the means of expression is created, works of similar form can be compared — for instance, the planar sculptures of Anton Pevsner and Alexander Calder. Clear distinctions can be found between such works, and one can perhaps come closer to understanding the premise of the individual sculptor, appreciating his particular use of the sculptural medium, and finally gaining insight into the meaning implicit in these works of art. Without such a method of organization, the typical museum visitor is faced with an almost impossible task, for, as we have stated earlier, the scope of contemporary expression is at once its strongest asset and its outstanding liability.

Modern Sculpture Series *(Figures 1-124 through 1-142)*

1—124

1—125

1-124 Intaglio Line: Josef Albers (1958) *intaglio Duo* (inkless intaglio engraving, printed without ink. 5-1/16 inches by 13-11/16 inches). (Collection, Museum of Modern Art, New York, Gift of Mr. and Mrs. Armand P. Bartos.)

1-125 Collage, Shape Composition with Low Texture: Kurt Schwitters *Merz (with Emerka Wrapper)* (1922) (collage of cut paper, carbon paper, mattress ticking). (Collection, Museum of Modern Art, New York, Katherine S. Dreier Bequest.)

1-128 Low Relief: Zoltan Kemeny (1957) *Miraculous Shadow* (copper mounted on wood, $33^5/_8$ inches by $21^7/_8$ inches). (Collection, Museum of Modern Art, New York, Gift of G. David Thompson.)

1-129 Middle Relief Assemblage: Louise Nevelson (1958) *Sky Cathedral* (painted wood construction, 11 feet $3^1/_2$ inches high, 10 feet $^1/_4$ inches wide, 1 foot 6 inches deep). (Collection, Museum of Modern Art, New York, Gift of Mr. and Mrs. Ben Mildwoff.)

1—128

1—129

1-126 Collage, Strong Texture: Leo Manso *Earth* (1962) (collage of painted fabric and paper, 23 inches by 20 inches). (Collection, Museum of Modern Art, New York, Gift of Dr. and Mrs. Ronald Neschi.)

1-127 Heavy Impasto, very Low Relief: Franco Assett. *Dark Seal,* 1958 (oil, partly in low relief on canvas, 35½ inches by 39⅜ inches). (Collection, Museum of Modern Art, New York, G. David Thompson Fund.)

1-130 High Relief: César (César Baldaccine, 1956) *Sculpture Picture,* (welded iron relief 20⅛ inches high, 39¾ inches wide, 8 inches deep). (Collection, Museum of Modern Art, New York, Gift of G. David Thompson.)

1-131 Environmental Relief: Jaap Wagemaker (1960) *Metallic Grey* (wood panel with aluminum egg slicer and scrap metal, painted, 24 inches by 19⅝ inches). (Collection, Museum of Modern Art, New York, Philip C. Johnson Fund.)

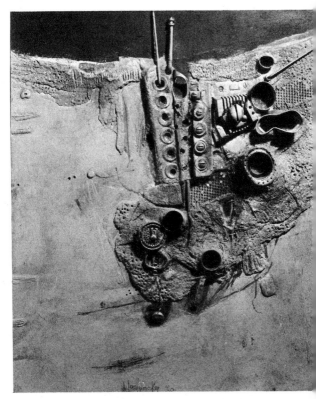

49

1-132 Environmental Sculpture, Base Predominant: Jean (Hans) Arp (1930) *Objects Arranged According to the Law of Chance or Navels* (varnished wood relief, 10³/₈ inches by 11¹/₈ inches). (Collection, Museum of Modern Art, New York, Purchase.)

1-133 Sculpture with Base, Equal Emphasis: Umberto Boccioni (1912) *Development of a Bottle in Space,* (bronze, 15 inches high). (Collection, Museum of Modern Art, New York, Aristide Maillol Fund.)

1-136 Concave-Convex Mass with Initial Penetration: Barbara Hepworth (1955-56) *Hollow Form* (Penwith) (lagoswood, partly painted, 36³/₈ inches high). (Collection, Museum of Modern Art, New York, Gift of Dr. and Mrs. Arthur Lejwa.)

1-137 Concave-Convex Mass with Extreme Penetration: Bruce Beasley (1960) *Chorus* (welded iron, 10¹/₂ inches by 14³/₄ inches). (Collection, Museum of Modern Art, New York, Gift of Mr. and Mrs. Frederick Weisman.)

1-134 Sculpture with Subordinate Base: Medardo Rosso (1892) *Man Reading*, (bronze, 10 inches high). (Collection, Museum of Modern Art, New York, Harry J. Rudick Fund.)

1-135 Monolithic Mass: Constantin Brancusi (1920, after a marble of 1915) *The New-Born* (bronze, 8¼ inches long, 5¾ inches high). (Collection, Museum of Modern Art, New York, Acquired through the Lillie P. Bliss Bequest.)

1-138 Highly Penetrated Mass: Theodore J. Roszak 1946-47) *Spectre of Kitty Hawk* (welded and hammered steel brazed with bronze and brass, 40¼ inches high). (Collection, Museum of Modern Art, New York, Purchase.)

1-139 Penetrated Mass with Developing Planar Surfaces: Henry Moore (1938) *Reclining Figure* (cast lead, 13 inches long). (Collection, Museum of Modern Art, New York, Purchase.)

1-140 Planar Form: Alexander Calder 1937) *Whale, Stabile* (sheet steel, 6 feet 6 inches high). (Collection, Museum of Modern Art, New York, Gift of the artist.)

1-141 Planar-Linear Form: Reg Butler (1952) *Woman Standing* (bronze and brass sheet and wire, welded, 18½ inches high). (Collection, Museum of Modern Art, New York, Acquired through the Lillie P. Bliss Bequest.)

1-142 Three-dimensional Linear Form: Ibram Lassaw 1952) *Kwannon* (welded bronze with silver, 6 feet high). (Collection, Museum of Modern Art, New York, Katharine Cornell Fund.)

1—140

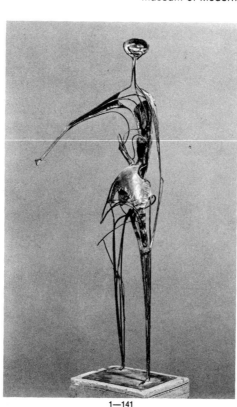

1—141

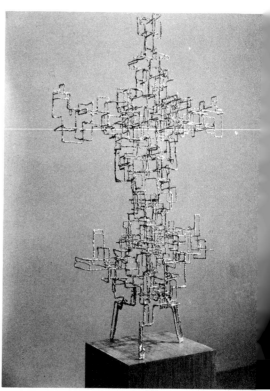

1—142

PART II. A DETAILED ANALYSIS:
Successive Stages of the Design Continuum

2—1 (above)   2—2 (below)

2—3 (above)   2—4 (below)

Line and Shape in a Two-Dimensional Space

Line:

A two-dimensional space can be defined most simply as a flat surface or plane with varying dimensions of height and width. Such a surface has been both the inspiration and despair for the thousands of generations of painters from the paleolithic caves of Altamira and Lascaux to the Bowery lofts of New York City today. A page of a newspaper, the surface of a quiet pond, the top of a sardine can, a painter's canvas, wallpaper, and a floor tile — all share the primary characteristic of a two-dimensional surface, namely, flatness.

The artist's task lies in the articulation of this empty, flat space. Perhaps the most primitive and possibly the most complex means for articulating a flat space is with a simple line. The introduction of this seemingly innocuous element into the naked void of two-dimensional space results in a shattering transformation. Suddenly the void no longer exists. One line has transformed space into two discernible areas. This process accelerates with the addition of further lines, as we see in Figures 2-1 and 2-2. Already the simple line has articulated the relatively flat surface of the water into hundreds of interrelated shapes. The isolation of areas can be described as one of the basic functions of line.

On a more sophisticated level, line reveals the inner nature of the artist; it becomes the handwriting of his most personal and intimate nature. Rembrandt's humanism seems most clearly expressed through

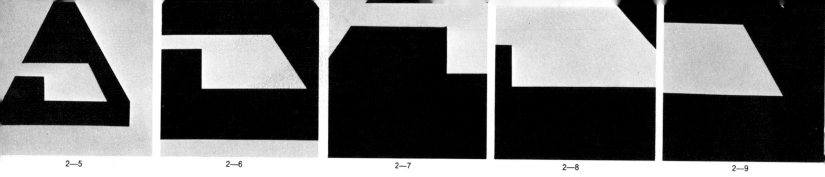

2—5   2—6   2—7   2—8   2—9

2-5 through 2-14 Variations on a Twodimensional Shape (Student project).

the medium of his drawings and etchings. Certainly our most trenchant recollection of Leonardo da Vinci is through his drawings. Goya reserved for the medium of graphic line his most anguished reflections on the human estate. The contrasts in character between artists such as Rouault, Matisse, Klee, Picasso, Pollack, and Kline is most clearly distinguishable through their use of line.

In another sense, the line drawing has a close affinity to chamber music as the most intimate form of expression within its own genre. For in both cases the artist cannot hide behind grandiose technique, subject matter, or other elegant subterfuges, which more elaborate means of expression afford. Therefore we place line as the very quintessence of Spartan means for the articulation of a two-dimensional space. The line is to drawing as the skeleton is to the human body, the vein to the leaf, or the cable to the suspension bridge.

It will suffice for the purposes of this discussion to allude to the infinite variety of forms that line can assume in a two-dimensional space: It can dissect a space with an austere and rigid formalism, as in Mondrian; it can titillate and amuse, as with Klee; it can seduce by its lyrical opulence, as with Botticelli; it can fill us with awe under the hand of a Hiroshige; it can strip an entire society of its pretense and hypocrisy when the artist is a Grosz, a Goya, or a Daumier; or it can turn us back toward life when the draftsman is a Matisse. Can we not conclude then that line is simultaneously man's most elemental and most abstract form of expression?

2-15 through 2-24 Variations on a Twodimensional Shape (Student project).

2—15   2—16   2—17   2—18   2—19

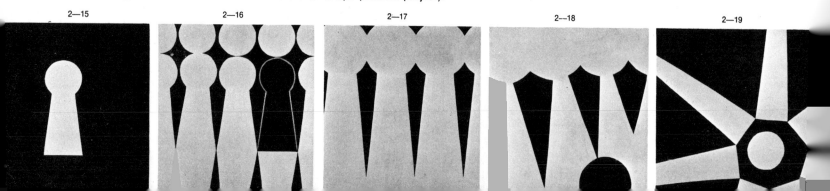

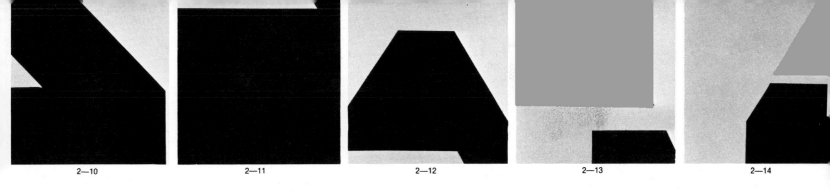

2—10   2—11   2—12   2—13   2—14

Shape:

The lower pair of related photographs on page 54 (Figs. 2-3 and 2-4) depicts, respectively, a close-up of the side of a zebra and a store front in Greenwich Village, New York City. In both cases we are confronted with an essentially flat plane that has been articulated by a series of shapes. Here the element of line in a two-dimensional space has been superseded by new visual elements — namely, value contrast and shape. In this new context the simple line has given way to solid areas of contrasting values, while the surface remains essentially flat. On the brick surface of the store front the scrawled existentialist linear message is virtually lost in the dominant, gray shapes of the brick background. The visual impact of these photographs derives from the contrast among the bold black, white, and gray shapes. Line has been subordinated to shape and value contrast; the reader may see this phenomenon by comparing the top pair of related linear photographs on page 54 (Figs. 2-1 and 2-2) to the bottom pair of shape photographs on the same page.

One of the most remarkable aspects of this sharp juxtaposition of values is the manner in which these contrasting shapes appear to rupture the sense of flatness and the integrity of the surface which we normally associate with a line on a two-dimensional plane. It is as if, with the introduction of value and shape, the eye no longer reads flatness. Instead it unconsciously assigns to one area or the other the

2—20   2—21   2—22   2—23   2—24

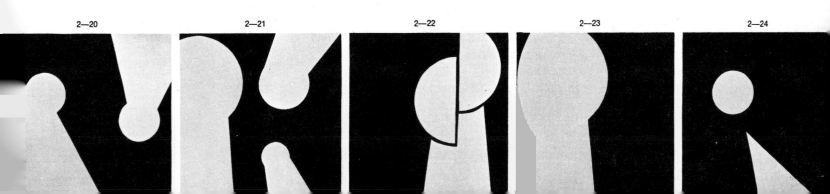

quality of projecting shape forward or backward in space — toward or away from the eye. If one concentrates on the photograph of the zebra's stripes for a few moments, he will notice that the white and black areas begin to undulate backward and forward in space. It becomes more and more difficult to know what is obvious: that both black and white shapes exist side by side in space on the same plane. This concept, two-dimensional figure-ground ambiguity, is also illustrated by Figure 2-35 (page 63) in the following section on two-dimensional illusory space. It is beyond the scope of this discussion to investigate the physiological and psychological phenomena within the apparatus of human vision which cause these apparent effects. The reader should, instead, refer to the excellent study by Rudolf Arnheim, *Art and Visual Perception;* William N. Dember's *Psychology of Perception;* and the clearly stated analysis of Op Art written by William C. Seitz, entitled *The Responsive Eye.*

If such relatively simple stimuli as juxtaposed black and white stripes of uniform size and shape can cause a major change in the appearance of a flat surface, it is not difficult to imagine what would happen to the spatial movement of black and white shapes if the artist were radically to alter their character by means of a series of variations similar to those seen in the photographs on pages 56 and 57. Notice how the mere alteration in scale, orientation, number, and value can affect the appearance and impact of these designs. These variations on a theme recall their musical counterparts, such as Bach's Goldberg Variations or the work in the fugue and variation genre of Handel, Mozart, Beethoven, and Bartok.

"More and more I excluded from my painting all curved lines, until finally my compositions consisted only of vertical and horizontal lines, which formed crosses, each one separate and detached from the other. Observing sea, sky, and stars, I sought to indicate their plastic function through a multiplicity of crossing verticals and horizontals.

"Impressed by the vastness of nature, I was trying to express its expansion, rest, and unity. At the same time, I was fully aware that the visible expansion of nature is at the same time its limitation; vertical and horizontal lines are the expression of two opposing forces; these exist everywhere and dominate everything; their reciprocal action constitutes 'life.' " Piet Mondrian, Plastic Art and Pure Plastic Art, page 13.

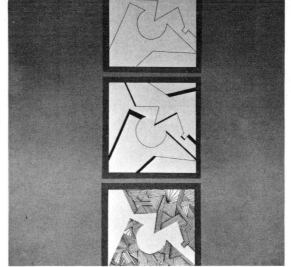

2—25

2—26

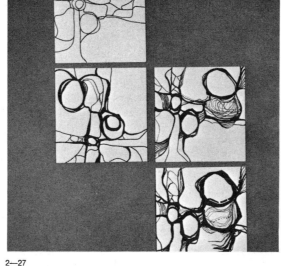

2—27

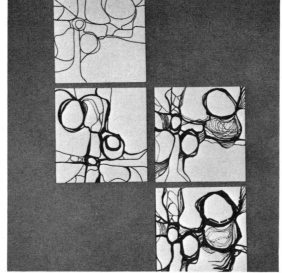

2—28

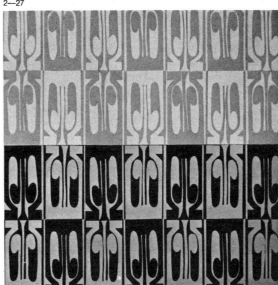

2—29 (above)   2—31 (below)

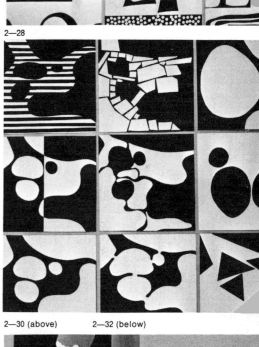

2—30 (above)   2—32 (below)

Student Projects (Figures 2-25 through 2-32)

2-25 Variations on a Two-dimensional Linear Composition.

2-26 Variations on a Two-dimensional Linear Composition.

2-27 Variations on a Two-dimensional Linear Composition.

2-28 Variations on a Two-dimensional Composition of Shapes.

2-29 Effects of Value and Chroma Change on a Two-dimensional Composition in Line and Shape.

2-30 Variations on a Two-dimensional Composition of Shapes.

2-31 Line and Shape Using Stained Glass Windows as a Design Source.

2-32 Analysis of a Masterwork: Shape and Three-Value Breakdown. Reversal of Values Study. Three-Chroma Breakdown.

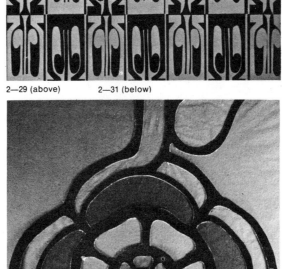

2-33 Architecture: Reflections on Times Square Store Front.
2-34 Nature: Photographic Composition.

Illusory Space: Painting

We must admire with genuine good humor man's obstinate and tenacious nature and zest for combat in the face of overwhelming odds in his long and uncompromising battle to overcome the essential flatness of a two-dimensional plane. No problem had plagued the artist more or, for that matter, drawn so heavily on the inner resources of his canny nature. The architect and the sculptor, being by temperament more practical men, simply appraised the impossibility of solving such a problem and directed their energies to the physical reality of three-dimensional space, abandoning as it were the enigma of two-dimensional spatial illusion to their more fanatic contemporaries.

In this brief discussion of *illusory space,* we will explore the incredible range of devices that man has employed to render space on a two-dimensional plane. The portable or semiportable two-dimensional surface has been available to a far greater number of artists, artisans, folk artists, and predatory iconoclasts than have the more expensive and exotic mediums of sculpture and architecture. A vast number of the artifacts of civilization were and are created in two-dimensional form, be it a tablet, parchment, paper, silk, canvas, newsprint, wood, metal, glass, or computer punch card.

It seems most germane to this discussion to examine the methods of *projection* that man has utilized from ancient times to the present to render the illusion of space. A projection within this context means an illusory extension beyond the normal surface of a two-dimensional plane — that is, the picture plane. With little apology for lack of consistent chronology, this discussion might begin with one of man's earliest methods of ordering a two-dimensional plane: *geometric projection.* This method makes little or no attempt to create an illusion of space. In fact its very means tend to maintain the integrity of the flat surface because of its preoccupation with clarity of symbolic expression. Word-picture language such as Egyptian hieroglyphics, Chinese and Japanese calligraphy, and American Indian symbolic languages have given birth to geometric forms of projection. Such forms tend to focus on scale in relationship to the importance of an object, rather than on spatial illusion. For example, the Egyptian artist represented the Pharaoh in a much larger scale than his courtly entourage; artisans and slaves were often represented as minuscule figures as befit their relative importance. Such devices as overlapping utilized to create the illusion of space in other projection methods were studiously avoided, for in geometric projection the symbolic content of the subject is of primary importance and the illusion of space relatively insignificant. Contemporary graphic techniques make generous use of this projection method. In its most refined state, the *grid* method, the projection is strictly geometric. Karl Gerstner's *Designing Programmes* is an excellent reference on this subject. The advertising art director's main task is to focus attention on objects in a given sequence; he is therefore quite willing to distort scale in favor of content, as did his predecessors two and three millenniums before the Christian era.

A second method by which man has attempted to render space is *parallel projection,* which was employed in classic Chinese and Japanese two-dimensional art forms. Some Western art historians have patronizingly referred to this projection method as a "primitive" method of rendering perspective space. They then proceed chauvinistically to illustrate its development by Western artists. More sophisticated art historians have suggested that the use of diagonal lines receding in parallel orientation was particularly appropriate to the art of scroll painting as practiced by the Chinese and Japanese masters. The diagonal emphasis of this projection method tended to move the eye through the unrolling space-time sequence of the scroll painting, anticipating, among other things, the motion picture. Thus parallel projection was an integral part of the esthetics of this art form. Needless to say, a one- or two-point perspective space would have arrested the very motion upon which the scroll painting depends for continuity.

During the Italian Renaissance, the spirit of scientific investigation led, as part of the immense acceleration of knowledge typical of the time, to the discovery of the science of one-, two-, and three-point perspective. Paolo Uccello, in his famous battle scenes, expressed his delight with this new discovery. Four centuries have not dimmed the Western artist's whimsical enthusiasm for the Florentine master's work — as witness Corrado Marca-Relli's canvas collage rendering homage to Uccello in The Metropolitan Museum of Art, New York City. It is not necessary to rehearse here the fascination that this new method of projection held for Masaccio, della Francesca, Mantegna, Raphael, and Leonardo; suffice it to say that its discovery became the anchorstone of naturalism in Renaissance painting. Ironically, in the late 19th century, a continuing allegiance to such outmoded methods of projection marked the true repository for stultified academic taste.

The term *plastic spatial projection,* an esthetic adjunct of the Renaissance perspective space, might be coined solely for the purposes of this discussion. The intent here is to relate to perspective space the extremely plastic representation of the human figure employed by such artists as Raphael, Michelangelo, Leonardo, and Bronzino. In such works the intent of the artist was to render the human figure in such a manner as to create a maximum illusion of three-dimensional form on a two-dimensional surface. Further discussion and visualization of this phenomenon are found in Part Three of this book (see Figs. 3-15 through 3-24, pages 120 and 121).

A direct evolution from perspective and plastic methods of projection led to the development of what has been termed *atmospheric perspective.* This projection method, while retaining linear perspective through a kind of shorthand, depended most heavily for its illusion of space on a diminishing amount of detail as objects receded in space. These "hazy" effects were the result of a direct observation of natural phenomena as they appear on cloudy and hazy days. Blurring of outlines is particularly associated with the Venetian School and the works of Titian, Giorgione, and Tintoretto. Such effects are sometimes referred to as "painterly," for the artist achieves spatial projection through the use of glazes, scumbling, and highly textured surfaces. Direct predecessors of this tradition in Western art would be such artists as Rubens, Watteau, Constable, and Turner. Joseph Turner's magnificently exuberant use of palette knife impasto in his wild seascapes and landscapes carried this genre of projection to its highest point of refinement.

In a category that might be called *color-space projection* can be grouped all the 19th- and 20th-century movements that employ the science of color phenomena wholly or in part to accentuate spatial illusion. Included in this general category are most of the Impressionists, the Post-Impressionists, the Pointillists, and the Geometric Abstractionists. If we can describe the Florentine scientist-painters of the Cinquecento as preoccupied with the discovery of perspective projection, we might be allowed the generalization that the main concern of the late 19th-century French school was with the science of color-space projection.

A kindred sense of excitement with scientific discovery infected the Impressionist painters. The writings of the French physicist and color theoretician Chevreul and his contemporaries were read with the enthusiasm of religious fanaticism; Science gave birth to Art for a young and iconoclastic generation of painters. The excitement that Monet, Renoir, Sisley, and Pissarro felt with the new tool of additive color mixtures through the use of juxtaposed primaries freed them from what they believed were the ponderous limitations of the subtractive palette. In this context, the subtractive palette describes the classical Western approach to color in which the artist mixes colors on his palette and then applies the mixture to his canvas. He may, for example, mix a primary red with a primary yellow to create the secondary orange, or mix green, a secondary color, with a primary blue to create the tertiary mixture of blue-green, and so on. Seurat, on the other hand, created color phenomena in a revolutionary fashion. Instead of mixing his colors subtractively on the palette, he used hundreds of tiny yellow, red, and blue dots placed in close proximity directly on the surface of the canvas in order to create color illusions. If he wished the observer to "see" the tertiary color blue-green in a certain area of a painting, Seurat used scientifically apportioned yellow and blue dots in that area. Theoretically, the optic nerve transmits the dot information from the retina to the brain where the actual mixture of the colors occurs. The resulting psychological or additive color mixture has a far greater immediacy and impact than the traditional subtractive color palette of the Renaissance and Baroque masters. This preoccupation with the science of color phenomena became a literal way of life for George Seurat and his followers. His Pointillist experiments were followed by the work of Van Gogh and Cézanne, the great color-space theoreticians Mondrian, Malevich, and finally the modern master of color, Josef Albers (see Josef Albers' *The Interaction of Color*). In the works of these men, psychological and physiological color space is explored to a very high degree of refinement. In general, the main goal of these artists has been to explore the extreme potentialities of spatial projection through the concentrated study of scientific color phenomena, optics, physiology, and psychology of human vision. In such studies the human eye is considered as the ultimate receptor of color stimuli. The psychology of perception, the various color-space theories of Munsell and Ostwald, and other related discoveries of contemporary physicists are utilized in the assault on this new frontier of two-dimensional spatial illusion. Even color evaluation instruments of considerable sophistication are employed, such as A. C. Hardy's spectrophotometer (see his *Handbook of Colormetry*). The contemporary Op Art movement serves as a direct extension from the work of Mondrian and Albers (see William Seitz's *The Responsive Eye*).

Another method of projection, peculiar to the 20th century, is the revolutionary *cubist-space* projection. We may still be too close to this movement fully to appreciate its incredible originality as a method of spatial projection. Cubist painters not only invented and refined the concept of the simultaneous view of an object, but began the fantastic exploration into the realm of spatial projection *out* from the picture plane towards the eye of the observer. Considering how much the 20th-century artist was influenced by these shattering experiments during the period 1907-1914, the importance of the Cubist discovery is not to be underestimated. Certainly its revolutionary spatial premise ranks as one of the greatest innovations in the entire history of art. A

2-35 Figure-Ground Continuum. Notice the subtle transition from figure area to ground area as the eye descends from the top to the bottom of this illustration.

direct creative outgrowth of early Cubist experimentation was the art of collage and assemblage — actual physical spatial projection (see Part Two, Section Three, *Textured Surfaces,* Pages 66-69).

Another revolutionary method of projection peculiar to the 20th century is the movement of Non-Objective Art, which had its germination in the work of Wassily Kandinsky. The premise of non-objective painting might be called that of an *infinite-space projection,* in which the so-called "picture-plane" is contemptuously discarded. The "window-in-space" concept, popular since the Renaissance, proved an anathema to these painters: They hoped to free painting from its last boundary — the tyranny of the frame. It is interesting to note in this respect that during the past 30 years the actual physical size of the picture frame has shrunk from that of the huge gold girdles of the 19th century to the pencil-thin strip. Arshile Gorky, Franz Kline, and Willem de Kooning used every device to project their non-objective images out in all directions from the picture plane, as if the painting itself were but a fleeting image in the infinity of an endless space.

In fairness to the diversity of spatial experimentation which characterizes the 20th-century artist, the *subjective-spatial projection* of the Surrealists and Expressionists should be mentioned. It is probably inaccurate to coin such a phrase in relation to the exploration of the inner reaches of man's nature; but perhaps the subjective character of the emotions and the unconscious mind will justify such an appellation. Again science led the way. As the studies of Sigmund Freud gained wider recognition, French poets and intellectuals, led by André Breton, were the first to realize what a cataclysmic effect these discoveries would have on the forms of art (André Breton, *Manifesto du Surréalisme-Poisson Soluble,* Paris, 1929).

In spite of the fact that the primary impact of Freud's work was to be felt by literary figures such as James Joyce, August Strindberg, Gertrude Stein, Franz Kafka, and Eugene O'Neill, it was inevitable that painters would respond to this stimulus as well. Hieronymus Bosch was rediscovered, James Ensor gained new converts, and belatedly even Salvador Dali joined in exploring the symbols of the unconscious mind, the realm of subjective space.

One final observation will suffice to close this abridged review of 25,000 years of man's attempts to render space on a two-dimensional plane. It is not inappropriate that we should close with a brief look at the most significant 20th-century method of projection, *motion picture space-time projection.* This most flexible of two-dimensional art forms expresses the ultimate in man's attempt to give the illusion of space to a two-dimensional plane. All of science and optical technology have been lent to perfecting the means of extending this illusion. We have seen recently the introduction and use of curved screens; simultaneous projection from several sources (Francis Thompson's *To Be Alive* and Charles Eames' *Think,* films at the New York World's Fair, 1964-65); 360-degree reflected projection and other devices that have attempted actually to move the spectator into the space of the picture plane. When we realize that the motion picture not only possesses the most sophisticated methods for representing spatial illusion but that as an esthetic vehicle it subtly combines drama, literature, music, the visual arts, dance, and mime into a space-time continuum, we can begin to appreciate its tremendous impact. It is clearly not only a means of communication, but an art form of inexhaustible range as well, the potential of which as a device for the extension of visual perception is still not fully realized. There is no doubt that this form of projection will lead to means as yet unexplored for assaulting the ageless enigma of endowing a flat surface with the illusion of space.

Student Projects (*Figures 2-36 through 2-55*)

2-36 Three-Value Neutral Breakdown of a Picasso Portrait (negative, tempera on mat board).

2-37 Three-Value Neutral Breakdown of a Picasso Portrait (positive, tempera on mat board).

2-38 Complementary Color Analysis of Manet's *Le Déjeuner Sur L'Herbe* (tempera on paper).

2-39 Two-Value Photostatic Breakdown of Manet's *Le Déjeuner Sur L'Herbe* (photostat).

2-40 Repeat Pattern Based on Egyptian Motif (tempera on paper).

2-41 Contemporary Motif on Monk's Cloth (tempera and dye on monk's cloth).

2-42 Cubist Collage (colored paper on mat board).

2-43 Collage (colored paper).

2-44 Collage (colored paper).

2-45 Figure-Ground Color Space (colored paper).

2-46 Color-Space Exercise (colored paper).

2-47 Op Art Experiment (colored tape on Plexiglas).

2-48 Relief Space (tempera on mat board).

2-49 Plastic Form (tempera on mat board).

2-50 Plastic Form (pastel).

2-51 Cubist Form (watercolor).

2-52 Surrealist Space (watercolor and pastel).

2-53 Surrealist Form (watercolor).

2-54 Expressionist Form (watercolor).

2-55 Surrealist Form in Space (pencil and ink).

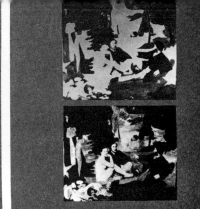

Above: 2—36 through 2—39

Below: 2—40 through 2—47.

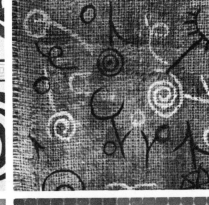

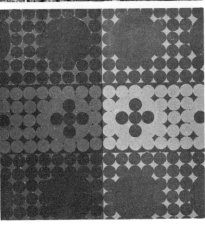

Below: 2—48 through 2—55

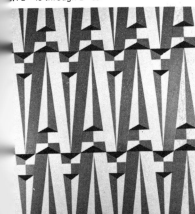

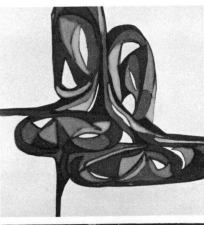
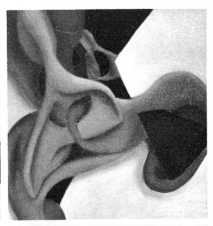

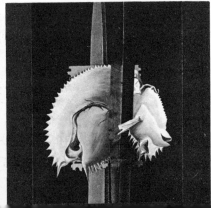

Textured Surfaces

Texture — the slight animation of a two-dimensional surface — can be considered as the first actual outward movement of form into a spatial environment. It is an active but not violent meeting of form and space. Texture may be seen everywhere, on the roofs of churches and in the humblest patch of earth (see Figs. 2-56 and 2-57). One chief characteristic of texture is its ability, because of its three-dimensional elements, to catch and model light. A second major characteristic is its "many-ness." In order for projections to be read as texture, there must be many units of form together. If there are so many of these units that the eye puts them all together instead of trying to read them individually, then a texture occurs. Think of the shingled roof on the opposite page. Seen from a distance of one or two feet, each shingle would be understood as a separate element of form next to another one like it. But from a greater distance, these smaller units blend into a textural whole. A third and perhaps the most important feature of texture is its tactile quality, which by itself should convey a sense of its subtle three-dimensional character. Whereas purely two-dimensional works appeal to our sense of sight alone, texture, with its definite projection into the third dimension, acts on both our sense of sight and our sense of touch. All the stages in the Design Continuum, from this point on, will share this tactile quality.

It is through mental associations with past tactile-visual experiences that we are able vicariously to enjoy texture wherever it appears. Thus our sight tells us of the roughness of the shingled roof without our actually touching the roof. In a highly puritanical society, the tactile sense is one of the first to be repressed. "Please Do Not Touch" signs echo throughout even the adult world. It is at once a refreshing note and a sad reminder of our present condition that certain contemporary sculptors ask the museum visitor to touch their work. The degree to which our tactile sense can be developed is no more apparent than in the swift, textural reading of the blind. It is unfortunate, to say the least, that our rich potential for tactile pleasure is so casually neglected, particularly when we consider how much we gain from our senses of sight, hearing, and taste.

Nature, as all of us have experienced, is filled with textures of infinite variety, from the roughness of a pineapple to the ripples in a quiet pond. But man, too, is an eloquent creator of textures — the peeling of paint unable to withstand the effects of time; the woven richness of Rya rugs in the hands of skilled Finnish craftsmen; the art of the plasterer who prepares interior walls for finishing; the architect whose skill in the selection of the final textural qualities of his materials can

2-56 Texture of Shingles on the Roof of a Church, Syracuse, New York.
2-57 Texture on the Floor of a Forest.

create a warm, human experience out of an otherwise calloused, superefficient building; and of course, the artist who utilizes textures not only as the heightened expression of a material he has selected, but also in the interpretation of ideas.

The use of texture in painting is perhaps as old as the art form itself. Egyptian encaustic painters utilized the layer-upon-layer nature of the medium to enrich their portraits texturally. The modular, tactile aspects of the mosaic tiled surfaces in the Roman Baths of Caracalla, Ostia Antica, and Pompeii are integral to and a function of the total esthetic impression. The tactile aspects of two-dimensional surfaces were explored even futher in the magnificent mosaic "tapestries" at Ravenna and Monreale. The mosaics were rendered transparent and framed with lead by Gothic stained-glass craftsmen. Thin linear bands of lead tracery combined with the inherent variations in the texture of the stained glass itself. The final effect presented a dramatic use of both color and texture.

The subtle texture of fresco was exploited to the full by Giotto and his school. With the introduction of the oil medium into Italy from Flanders in the late quattrocento, a new and infinitely subtle method for utilizing texture was made available to the easel painter. The flexibility of the new medium, notably in the use of glazing, impasto, and *alla prima* techniques, can be traced through the works of Titian and Caravaggio to Rubens and Rembrandt. Rembrandt's use of wax to heighten impasto areas led to the technique of tactile accentuation which became the stand-by of such 19th-century artists as Turner, Constable, and Courbet.

During the 19th century, with the possible exception of Courbet, van Gogh stands out as having carried to the ultimate the expressive potential of texture on a two-dimensional surface. He introduced a low-relief textural quality into his heavily impastoed paintings. Thick applications of pigment created highlights and shadows that intensified the color and, consequently, the entire picture surface. The picture surface began to break loose from its two-dimensionality and emerged upwards into space.

As in other areas, it was left to the 20th-century artist to exploit fully this aspect of painting. The qualities of texture have nowhere been better expressed than in the contemporary art form of collage or assemblage, wherein an effort was made by the artist to select and combine various materials. The early contributions of Braque, Picasso, and Schwitters led to the bolder experiments of Mansu, Burri, Marca-Relli, and Rauschenberg.

The technique of collage and of texture in general serves as a clear transition from two-dimensional painting and illusory space to the physical actuality of relief.

"Like abstract art, however, the most characteristic assemblage occupies real space. Physically, its method can be as direct as filling a cupboard or setting a dinner table. Herein lies one outcome of Cubism's dialectic between illusion and actuality: Formerly, the space and form of painting was physically false, and that of sculpture physically real. Cubism closed the painted picture-window to make of it the painting-object: A part of the environment that projects quite naturally into three dimensions. Questioned in Paris as to why he had added objects to his painting, Robert Rauschenberg answered, 'Paint itself is an object, and canvas also. In my opinion, the void which must be filled does not exist.'" (William C. Seitz, *The Art of Assemblage,* page 25.)

"Here is the parting of the ways. A step further and the picture, and with it the effort to fathom the object by the graphic method, would disappear. The next treatment would have to be: to mount the object itself, in whole or in section, in its original size, on a board." Laszlo Moholy-Nagy, The New Vision, *pages 35 and 36.*

". . . it is often very difficult in any given case to disssociate entirely our visual reactions from our tactile reactions. Even when one organ is not directly involved, as when we look at a surface, a whole series of associations based on the tactile knowledge of surfaces may be aroused." Herbert Read, The Art of Sculpture, *page 70.*

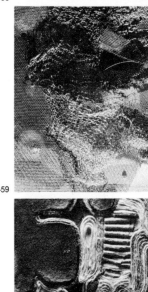

2—58

2—59

2—60

2—61

Student Projects *(Figures 2-58 through 2-63)*

2-58 Collage of Seeds, String, and Sand.

2-59 Collage of Wire Screen and Gravel.

2-60 Collage of Yarn, Fabric, and Hemp.

2-61 Collage of Painted String Stylizing Butterfly Wings.

2-62 Collage of Painted, Knotted Hemp Interpreting the Texture and Color of Indian Corn.

2-63 Textural Composition in Plaster.

2—62

2—63

2-64 Low Relief: Kaufmann Camp-grounds Pools, Upstate New York. Designed by Edward Larrabee Barnes, Architect. (Photograph courtesy of the architect.)
2-65 Low Relief: Detail, Winter Landscape.

2-66 Middle Relief: Mural of Soccer Players, University of Mexico, Mexico City.
2-67 Middle Relief: Snow Landscape.

2—64 (above)

2—66 (below)

Relief

Relief is a clear transitional form between the painter's two-dimensional space and the world of three dimensions; it contains elements from both these areas of visual form. From the flat two-dimensional world, relief retains the basic idea of a surface, a frontal plane, within which there is movement into space. Sometimes, as in Ghiberti's

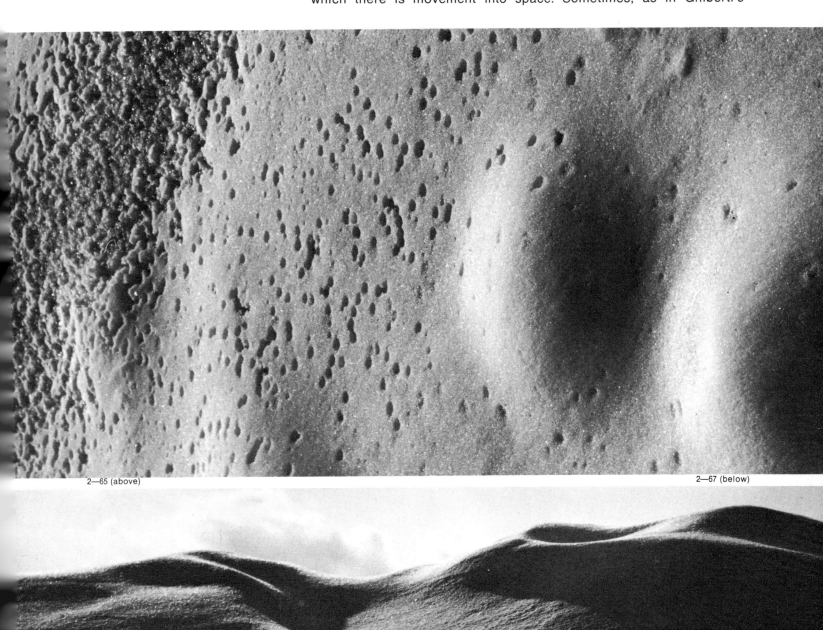

2—65 (above)

2—67 (below)

Doors of Paradise in Florence, the painter's space with its illusions of recession was actually emulated by the relief sculptor. Relief, as Herbert Read remarks, "confines the senses within a pictorial framework" (Herbert Read, *The Art of Sculpture,* page 56).

But importantly, relief is the two-dimensional conception interpreted in an increasingly three-dimensional manner with a distinct emphasis on its three-dimensional qualities. The aspect of the third dimension in relief is basic to our understanding of this visual form. Texture made use of light to animate a surface, creating the infinite number of highlights and shadows which we read as physical texture. In relief the role of light as a surface modulator is even more crucial. The physical movement of a surface into space obviously presents a greater opportunity for light to strike the surface at more points and from a variety of directions. Basically, those surfaces perpendicular to and facing the falling rays of light will be lightest in value, receiving and reflecting the most light, while those surfaces lying away from the light will be darkest in value. By adjusting the angle of the surfaces in a relief, the artist can orchestrate a surface with all the middle gray values plus white and black. Light and its absence in shadow thus acts as the catalyst and vehicle for the articulation of the surface of the relief.

Perhaps the key to understanding relief is the idea of the integrity of a surface. A feeling for this concept may be gained by a simple mental experiment. Consider starting at the edge of a relief with a pencil in hand and moving the pencil point in any direction along the surface of the relief. The condition of relief may be defined as permitting us to move the pencil completely across, up, and over the surface. Thus though the surface physically projects or recedes into space, no portions of it are completely three-dimensional. This conception deviates from the commonly accepted definition of relief, which would describe Roman friezes (see Fig. 1-37 on page 28) as high relief even though portions of the figures are fully three-dimensional. By creating new form categories for friezes like this (*environmental relief* or *environmental sculpture*), there will be less ambiguity in discussions about relief and consequently greater understanding of this rich visual form.

Figure and ground relationships in relief can be spoken of whether we are considering basically concave reliefs, in which there is a movement of the surface inwards away from the observer, or convex reliefs, in which areas of the surface project toward the observer. In the typical relief some areas of the surface advance and some recede from what is perceived as a "neutral plane." These advancing or receding portions model the impinging light more strongly than the neutral plane and consequently begin to be seen as "figures" in a less articulated, more neutral "ground."

> "There would be various types of depth relief: The total relief might be concave, with the objects in the center lying at the greatest distance, or — on the contrary — a convex relief might build up a protrusion in the center. The factor of interruptedness versus coherence could be studied in both the frontal and the depth dimensions. In some works a continuous 'chromatic' scale of levels would lead from the front toward the back, whereas in others there would be large intervals, for example, between foreground and background." (Rudolf Arnheim, *Art and Visual Perception,* page 189.)

The intensity of separation between the various levels in the relief creates conditions known as low, middle, and high relief. A relief in

2-68 High Relief: Casa Mila ("La Pedrera") Barcelona. Detail of façade (1905-07), designed by Antoni Gaudi. Photographed by Herbert Brooks Walker. (From Art Nouveau exhibit, Museum of Modern Art, New York, 1960. Photograph courtesy, the Museum of Modern Art.)
2-69 High Relief: Composition of Exposed Tree Roots.

which there appears almost no separation of planes, such as the Egyptians produced, is low relief.

"The technique was one of incision, essentially linear, essentially graphic. Egyptian sculpture was made to be read, like the Egyptian pictorial script." (Herbert Read, *The Art of Sculpture,* page 54.)

Besides the incised reliefs, the Egyptians created low reliefs that projected just enough to model the edge of the emerging forms (see Fig. 1-35, pages 26 and 27). These low or bas-reliefs read as quite flat surfaces, a primarily ground condition (see Figs. 2-64 and 2-65, pages 70 and 71).

In middle relief the separation of planes becomes even more pronounced. The relation between figures and ground equalizes, and the emerging or receding areas attract attention to a greater degree (see Figs. 2-66 and 2-67).

High relief carries the movement of the surface into space to its most extreme limits while still preserving the integrity of the surface. The figure elements appear to be attempting to free themselves from the surface and give the impression of some inner force pushing and deforming the surface into space (see Figs. 2-68 and 2-69, page 72).

Student Projects *(Figures 2-70 through 2-85)*
2-70 Low Relief: Heavy Paper.
2-71 Low Relief: Carved Fibre board.
2-72 Low Relief: Discarded Chewing Gum Packages.
2-73 Low Relief: Modular Paper Sculpture Composition.

2-74 Middle Relief: Plaster.
2-75 Middle Relief: Tooled Copper Sheet.
2-76 Middle Relief: Modular Paper Sculpture Composition.
2-77 Middle Relief: Wood.
2-78 Middle Relief: Plaster.
2-79 Middle Relief: Reverse Plaster Cast of Figure 2-78.
2-80 Middle Relief: Plaster.
2-81 Middle Relief: Reverse Plaster Cast of Figure 2-80.

2-82 High Relief: Plaster, positive relief with Reverse Casting.
2-83 High Relief: Modular Paper Sculpture Composition.
2-84 High Relief: Formed Copper Sheet.
2-85 High Relief: Plaster, Positive Relief with Reverse Casting.

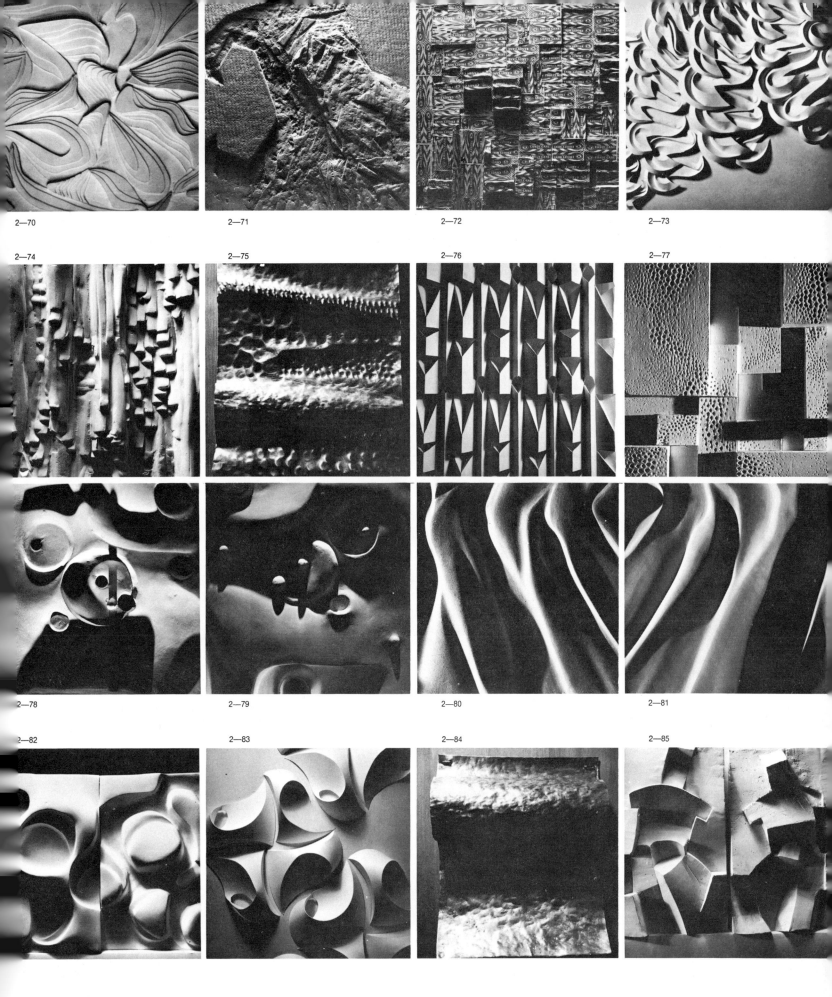

2—70   2—71   2—72   2—73

2—74   2—75   2—76   2—77

2—78   2—79   2—80   2—81

2—82   2—83   2—84   2—85

Environmental Relief

At this point it is necessary for the reader to re-evaluate and enlarge his concept of relief. In the last section the integrity of the surface as a basic condition of relief was stressed. The reader should now consider the relief as a kind of environment for small, emerging three-dimensional ground forms, which may or may not interrupt the continuity of the surface. These ground forms are subordinate to the environmental relief. They are like dwellings set in a much larger, encompassing landscape. In the photographs on the opposite page — a natural snow formation and the excavations of a triumphal road in Egypt — there is a general feeling for a relief-like environment created by small bumps and depressions in the surface of the snow and by the terracing and unevenness of the terrain in excavation. Within the relief environment of the snow, there appear a number of snow forms that are distinctly three-dimensional in character, especially those toward the upper center of the photograph. In the architectural photograph we note this same condition: the foundations of the ruins to the right and particularly in the procession of sphinx statues. In both cases, however, these emerging forms never dominate the environment but interact with it to form a visual whole.

Forms of this condition may be frequently seen in natural landscapes with emerging tree stumps, boulders, knolls, or bushes, but the sharpest analogy may be found in architecture and city planning. One need look no farther than the countless housing developments that rape our landscape to get a feeling for the large flat or rolling environment with three-dimensional forms of houses scattered over its surface. The passive relationship between form and environment, house and landscape, in these developments creates a condition of visual boredom and monotony. Far more exciting visually are attempts by architects at establishing either a sharply contrasting or intimately organic relationship between the dwelling and its much larger environment. Marcel Breuer creates a dynamic tension between his houses and their environment by deliberately creating rigid forms and using primary color accents to contrast with the more fluid forms and subtler colors found in the natural sites of his architecture. Frank Lloyd Wright took quite the opposite approach in his concept of "organic architecture."

"Garden and building may now be one. In any good organic structure it is difficult to say where the garden ends and where the house begins or the house ends and the garden begins — and that is all as should be, because Organic architecture declares that we are by nature ground-loving animals, and insofar as we court the ground, know the ground and sympathize with what it has to give and produce in what we do to it, we are utilizing practically our birthright." (Frank Lloyd Wright, *Organic Architecture*, page 12.)

And again Wright proclaims:

"The Usonian house, then, aims to be a natural performance, one that is integral to site; integral to environment; integral to the life of the inhabitants. A house integral with the nature of materials — wherein glass is used as glass, stone as stone, wood as wood — and all the elements of environment go into and throughout the house. . . .

"Into this new integrity, once there, those who live in it will take root and grow. And most of all belonging by nature to the

2-86 Environmental Relief: Egyptian Excavations. (Photograph courtesy of the United Arab Republic Tourist and Information Center. Photographer C. Zacharv.)
2-87 Environmental Relief with Emerging Ground Forms: Detail, Winter Landscape.

nature of its being." (Frank Lloyd Wright, *The Natural House*, pages 134 and 135.)

Certainly the architectural works of Wright testify to his concept — the Kaufmann "Falling Water House" at Bear Run, Pennsylvania; Taliesin West and East; the Johnson House at Racine, Wisconsin, to mention but a few. It is interesting to note that in the Guggenheim Museum in New York City Wright created an architecture that was organic within itself but, like Marcel Breuer, chose to place it in direct contrast with the surrounding environment. The result was a vigorous departure from the Park Avenue glass boxes.

One can readily extend this analogy to the environment of a city in relation to its visual component forms. Seen from an airplane the city becomes a huge relief. Fire hydrants, street lights, benches, pools and fountains, sidewalk carts and vendors, automobiles, and people become the environmental forms within the relief. The interaction of these elements with the city environment is seen as a very real art form by Lawrence Halprin.

The comparison of snow-scene and cityscape again asserts that visual form is independent of scale and is purely a function of our frame of reference. With this viewpoint, it is possible for the observer to seek and understand visual form not only in museums, gardens, and grandiose natural scenery, but in the very cityscapes wherein he dwells. An awareness of the basic architectural premise of relating a building to its site in the more abstract sense of form in an environment will help to make the reader conscious of similar relationships in other areas — in the arrangement of furniture in a room, paintings hung on a wall, objects set on a table, a brooch on a woman's dress, and even icing and candles on a birthday cake!

"The first great consideration is that life goes on in an environment; not merely in it but because of it, through interaction with it." John Dewey, Art as Experience, page 13.
". . . as the developing growth of an individual from embryo to maturity is the result of interaction of organism with surroundings." Ibid., page 28.

"Finally the city comes alive through movement and its rhythmic structure. The elements are no longer merely inanimate. They play a vital role, they become modulators of activity and are seen in juxtaposition with other movement flows, the paving and ramps become platforms for action, the street furniture is used, the sculpture in the street is seen and enjoyed. And the whole city landscape comes alive through movement as a total environment for the creative process of living." Clarence Halprin, Cities, page 9.

"Throughout the natural world we find a close structural correspondence between the form of an organism and the character of its surroundings, whether in the earthworm or in any other living thing." Norman Newton, An Approach to Design, page 134.

2-88 Taliesin West: Frank Lloyd Wright, architect. (Photograph, Pedro E. Guerrero.)

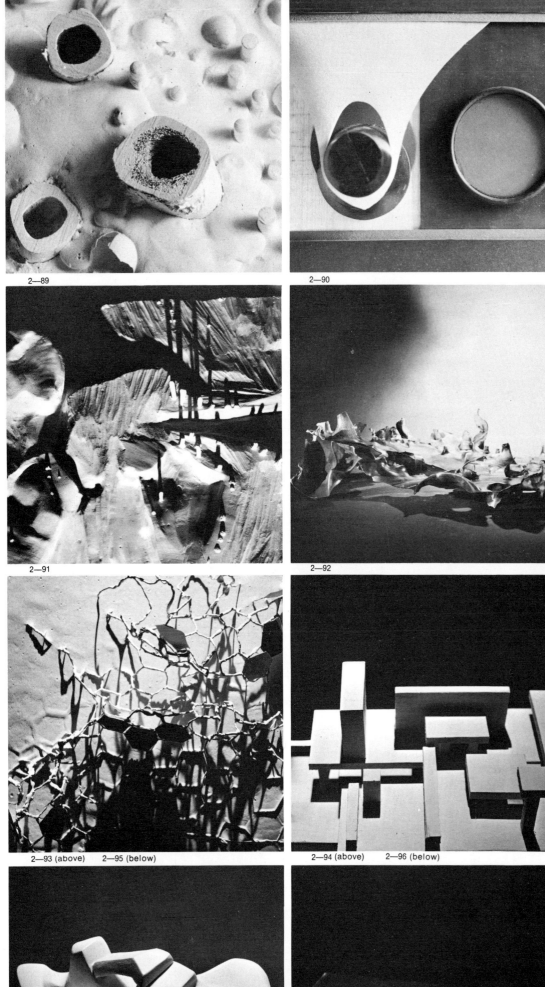

2—89

2—90

2—91

2—92

2—93 (above)   2—95 (below)

2—94 (above)   2—96 (below)

Student Projects *(Figures 2-89 through 2-96)*

2-89 Environmental Relief: Bones, Plaster, Egg Shell, and Chalk.

2-90 Environmental Relief: Rubber Products.

2-91 Environmental Relief: Plaster and Matchsticks.

2-92 Environmental Relief: Heat-formed Plastic.

2-93 Environmental Relief: Chicken Wire and Painted Cardboard.

2-94 Environmental Relief: Wood.

2-95 Environmental Relief: Plaster.

2-96 Environmental Relief: Plaster.

2-97 Environmental Sculpture: Chimneys of Cave Dwellings, Gaudix, Spain. (Photograph, Myron Goldfinger, architect.)

2-98 Environmental Sculpture: Temple of Abu Simbel, Egypt, at the original site on the Nile before removal for the Aswan Dam project. Built 3200 years ago under Pharaoh Rameses II. Height of figures, 65 feet. (Photograph courtesy of the American Committee to preserve Abu Simbel.)

2-99 Environmental Sculpture: Rock and Wood Formation.

"Simple circles and ovals also appear. A quality of dynamic life is imparted to the groups of related shapes by variations in size and scale. The emphasis on empty background areas throws into sharp relief and lends new proportions to the contrasting forms. Within the 'boundlessness of the plane surface' (which seems to exist as an aspect of infinity), every formal event is enhanced, its dimensions sharpened, to become, for the eye, a new and universal alphabet of basic shapes." Museum of Modern Art, Arp, page 21.

Environmental Sculpture

Once the concept of relief as an environment is grasped, it is relatively easy to discuss the relationship of the environmental relief to the sculptural ground forms on its surface. In the last section the relief was considered as the dominant feature of the total visual composition, whereas the forms were very subordinate. In this section the environmental relief and the sculptural forms will be, compositionally, of equal importance.

This visual condition may be termed *environmental sculpture,* because at this point in the Continuum the emerging form has the distinct characteristics of full three-dimensional sculpture and is seen as such in combination with a relief environment. There is an ambiguity of emphasis here in which form and physical environment (relief) are struggling with each other for visual dominance. One of the clearest and best-known examples of this visual form are the XIX Dynasty Egyptian figures at the temple of Abu Simbel. The 65-foot-high figures on the opposite page (Fig. 2-98) are clearly three-dimensional but exist in conjunction with a chamberlike environment in the side of a large cliff. The texture of the cliff is slight compared to the powerful, rounded forms of the figures, but the cliff itself is huge. Consequently neither the figures nor the cliff dominates. Herbert Read has an interesting comment on this type of form-environment composition.

"If we turn to the sculpture of Egypt we find a similar predominance of relief sculpture, and even when the statues are in the round they are often supported by a background. . . . A . . . plausible explanation is provided . . . by a consideration of the function of sculpture in Egypt. It was never regarded as a separate and distinct art. From the beginning it was subordinate to architecture and the nature of the architecture determined the nature and even the technique of the sculpture." (*The Art of Sculpture,* page 51.)

2-100 New York Cityscape.

He further states that ". . . the Egyptian sculptor had no desire to isolate the human figure in space, to disassociate it from its niche or socket, for to do so would have served no rational purpose." (*Ibid.,* page 53.)

Architecture again affords some of the richest examples of environmental sculpture. The photograph on the opposite page (Fig. 2-97) pictures chimneys of cave dwellings in Gaudix, Spain. Resembling miniature lighthouses, their strong cylindrical forms emerge from the hillside in a strange combination of form and environment. Another more well-known architectural work is Versailles, in which a huge French palace has been juxtaposed with a formal garden of tremendous scale.

> "What is the significance of Versailles? What is the important constituent fact it embodies? It is the close contact it effects with nature. An immense complex of buildings, more than two thousand feet long, has been directly confronted with nature; the grounds are a real part of the structure itself, and form with it a whole of great power and grandeur." (Sigfried Giedion, *Space, Time and Architecture;* page 72.)

Certainly one of the most dramatic examples of this type of visual form occurs in the cityscape of New York (Fig. 2-100, page 82). Seen from across the East River, the older skyscrapers, all relatively the same height, merge to form a spiny environment. From this environment rise the newer structures of incredible height, with the towering smokestacks along the East River projecting dramatically in the foreground. It is difficult to imagine a clearer statement of environmental sculptures than these.

"For in all we do as [architectural] designers we are seeking to create forms — environmental forms in which humans may carry on some one or more of the many activities that constitute living." Norman Newton, An Approach to Design, *page 131.*

2—101

2—102

Student Projects *(Figures 2-101 through 2-104)*
2-101 Environmental Sculpture: Wood.
2-102 Environmental Sculpture: Plaster.
2-103 Environmental Sculpture: Wood.
2-104 Environmental Sculpture: Papier-mâché and Paper.

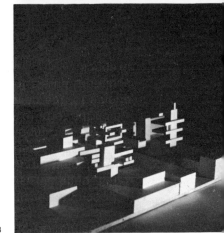

2—104

2—103

2-105 Sculpture with Base: Auditorium, New York University. (Marcel Breuer, architect, Photograph, Ben Schnall.)
2-106 Sculpture with Base: Natural Earth Formation.
2-107 Sculpture with Base: Twin Chapel, Mykonos, Greece. (Photograph by architect Myron Goldfinger.)

2—106

2—107

Sculpture with Base

Easily one of the most dynamic stages in the Design Continuum, the idea of a sculpture with a base captures the emerging three-dimensional sculptured form at the point where it is almost freed from its relief environment. The visual emphasis in the composition is now on the three-dimensional form, and the base is subordinate (the opposite condition, it should be noted, to environmental relief). This is the point in the Design Continuum immediately preceding monolithic form and as such occupies a key transitional position in the total spectrum of visual form. The three-dimensional sculpture exists primarily in an environment of *space*, which is to be its home from this point on. But the concept of a base on a three-dimensional form is not to be overlooked as merely a superfluous appendage. It is a vital part of the entire composition and influences to a great extent the character of the three-dimensional form above it. Witness the comment opposite by the sculptor Henry Moore.

It is very clear from the three accompanying photographs on the opposite page that this expression of visual form is hardly limited to sculpture, although some of the most provocative of sculptural works have assumed this character. The ancient twin church on the Greek island of Mykonos (Fig. 2-107) bears a striking similarity in visual form composition to the auditorium at New York University designed by Marcel Breuer (Fig. 2-105). Both works of architecture are powerful geometric forms dominating a setting that is visually and physically a base for the structure. Nature, too, provides numerous examples, such as the eroded hillside in the third photograph (Fig. 2-106).

In the field of sculpture, artists like Rodin, Medardo Rosso, and Boccioni attempted to solve the visual problem of emerging three-dimensional forms. Rodin's remarkable series of hands thrust upward from rough stone. The contrast between the expressive, finely carved hands and the harshly modeled base creates a striking composition. One can find similar conceptual solutions in the work of Medardo Rosso. As a sculptor, Rosso was very aware of the ambience, or surrounding space environment, which he attempted to express in his pieces. This expression took two directions (see Fig. 1-134, page 51). The first was a more impressionistic development of the surface, resulting in an atmospheric interaction between sculpture and space at their common boundary. The second was a feeling for forms that emerge from a base as an environment. The "base" is often vaguely articulated in Rosso's works, and there is usually a very organic and fluid transition between the emerging full sculptural forms and their physical environments.

"What Boccioni admired in Rosso," suggests Margaret Scolari Barr, "was the impinging pressure of the environment upon the subject and the extension of the subject into its surroundings." (Margaret Scolari Barr, *Medardo Rosso,* page 63.) It is clear from Boccioni's own work during the Futurist period in Italy (see Fig. 1-133, page 50) that his concerns were very similar to those of Rosso, though Boccioni replaced the impressionistic quality of Rosso's work with stronger, more architectural forms.

> "The Futurists . . . looked upon all objects, in fact, whether a static bottle or a racing horse, as embodying two kinds of motion; that which tends to move in on itself, suggesting in its centripetal force the internal mass of an object; and that which moves outward into space mingling its rhythms with those of other objects and eventually merging with space itself." (Joshua Taylor, *Futurism,* page 12.)

Boccioni's fascinating sculpture *Evolution of a Bottle in Space* (Fig. 1-133, page 50) is one of the most conceptually perfect examples of a developing form, pushing outwards from a base into space. There is a tight visual interrelation between the base and the "bottle." But of even greater import is the expression of emergence and development which the form reveals. If we accept Boccioni's premise, there is little choice for the next stage in the evolution of form — one in which the sculpture bursts free of its bonds and stands isolated as a pure form in space.

"But even apart from such an evolutionary explanation, it is a natural instinct to give an object a base; even a painter generally seeks his horizon line, or some reference to solid ground. The sculptor has the very practical consideration of stability; that is to say, if he is a naturalistic sculptor, and wants his figure to stand, he must replace the muscular tensions which keep the living model on its feet by a solid block of some sort to which the figure's feet are securely attached. This may seem a trivial observation, but it is a fact which has distorted the whole development of sculpture in its naturalistic phase. For the base has inevitably shifted the centre of gravity of the sculptured object; indeed, the object has in itself lost its true centre of gravity and in the physical sense becomes merely a protuberance from a substantial mound of some sort." (David Sylvester, Henry Moore, pages X and XI.)

2—108

2—109

2—110

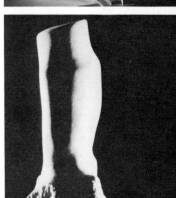

2—111

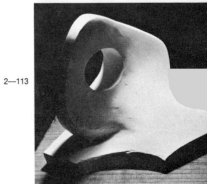

2—112

Student Projects *(Figures 2-108 through 2-113)*
2-108 Sculpture with Base: Copper.
2-109 Sculpture with Base: Pumice Stone.
2-110 Sculpture with Base: Copper and Wood.
2-111 Sculpture with Base: Wood.
2-112 Sculpture with Base: Sculp-Stone.
2-113 Sculpture with Base: Plaster.

2—113

2-114 Monolithic Mass: Joseph E. Seagram Building,New York City. (Photograph courtesy of Joseph E. Seagram
and Sons, Inc.)
2-115 Monolithic Mass: Sea Shell.

Monolithic Mass

"When we free our figure elements from a physical ground, a
new condition arises. As far as our visual pattern is concerned,
we still perceive the form because of figure-ground organization. The contrast between material and space defines the
form. But now the ground can no longer be thought of as a
physical part of the pattern. . . ." (Robert Scott, *Design Fundamentals,* page 136.)

Though any three-dimensional form satisfies Scott's description, a
monolithic form is perhaps the purest statement of a three-dimensional
figure-ground, form-space relationship. A monolith can be considered
as absolute three-dimensional form, closed and complete. No vestiges
of its attachment to a physical environment remain. It could as well be
floating in space like a dirigible as be at rest on a surface. It is isolated
mass, resisting the intrusion of space and almost arrogant in its relation to other forms. It represents the point in our Continuum where
form has emerged as a total physical entity.

It is not difficult to find examples of monolithic form. A towering
skyscraper like the Seagram Building, though lightened by reflections
off its surfaces (exactly as in the mirrorlike finishes of many of Brancusi's sculptures), remains powerful in its statement of a closed geometric form. The ancient Egyptian pyramids present to an even greater
degree almost imponderable mass. Natural elements such as tree
stumps, sea shell forms, boulders, and fruits like oranges or grapefruit may be viewed as monolithic forms.

Monolithic form may be considered the first stage in the process of
carving, or subtractive sculpture. It is the pure, untouched block from
which the sculptor extracts his final sculptural form. Michelangelo
spoke of "liberating forms from the marble block." His remarkable
Captive Slaves bear silent witness to this as they struggle to extricate

themselves from the stone that engulfs them. Those sculptural works that reflect the integrity of the solid block are generally the most monolithic in character. The Mayans, Egyptians, and Africans made only slight penetrations into the block to create the suggestion of form. Hildebrand described this process in his study on *The Problem of Form:*

> "Likewise primitive sculpture in the round may be easily looked upon as a result of surface drawing carved into a block. Thus the ancient Egyptians carved crouching figures out of blocks of stone, maintaining in the process the original bounding surfaces of the stone, yet converting it into members of a crouching figure. The stone was first roughly cut into a simple general form, and this form was then modified according to the figure intended. The block is thus changed into a human figure; and, indeed, from a certain distance we might readily take such a block for such a figure. In the statue the stone is no longer a stone, but continues to exist, nevertheless, as the total form of the figure. . . . The original block gave the illusion of a crouching figure; the crouching figure irresistibly suggests the original block." (Adolf Hildebrand, *The Problem of Form,* page 125.)

There have been a number of contemporary sculptors whose work has been directly influenced by, or at least reflects to a great degree, early monolithic forms. Henry Moore, many of whose nonpenetrated reclining figures or groups are strongly monolithic, tells us of his interest in these "primitive" forms. Similarly, the sculptural austerity of Modigliani's heads suggests an interest in preserving the integrity of the block. "The kinship, however, is not to be sought in any borrowing of form, but rather in a similar means of stressing essential volumes." (Carola Giedion-Welcker, *Contemporary Sculpture,* page 38.)

The modern sculptor who has created the most visually subtle and conceptually powerful statements of monolithic form is unquestionably Constantin Brancusi. His concern for the purest expression of three-dimensional form is evident in practically every work he created (see Fig. 1-135, page 51). Yet these sculptures, in all their purity, are far from lifeless and sterile. They reveal minute shifts in the axis of the volumes and in the swelling of various portions of the sculpture as it is rotated. More than this, however, Brancusi polishes his metal sculptures to a smooth and highly reflective finish. The surface thus responds to other objects in the environment by re-creating them in a pattern that aids in the definition of the form. The mirrored environment reflected by the surface serves to lighten the form by creating an illusory feeling of space that appears to penetrate the solid form.

Monolithic form might, in conclusion, be divided into two major areas. The first consists of forms whose surfaces are relatively inanimate — neither highly textured to model light nor highly reflective, such as an egg. These are most expressive of solid, impenetrable mass. The second area contains forms like the Seagram Building or Brancusi's metal sculptures, whose surfaces reflect objects in the surrounding environment. The illusory penetration of space into the monolith by means of these reflections suggests the first subtle step in the deterioration of mass which will occupy the remaining stages of the Continuum. In a cyclical manner suggesting the first portion of the Design Continuum one can, having examined illusory space, study the effects of texture and relief on the solidity of a monolithic form. The application of relief to the monolith is the topic of the next section.

"Their transparency becomes transcendence. *Not only do they receive through this process the faculty of capturing and emitting light, but they are also given a spatial and spiritual force of emanation that is particularly intense. By sheer virtue of its high polish the self-enclosed form-kernel opens up to space, illuminates it and takes mirrored possession of it and the surrounding world on every side." Carola Giedion-Welcker,* Brancusi, *page 25.*

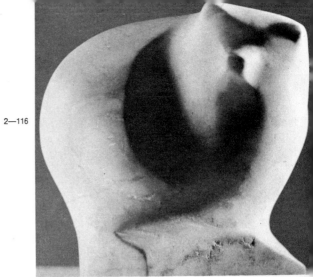

2—116

2—117

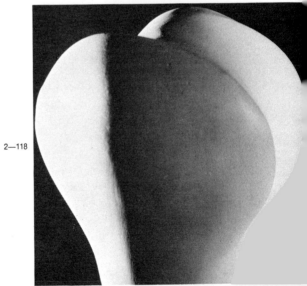

2—118

Student Projects *(Figures 2-116 through 2-119)*
2-116 Monolithic Mass: Sculp-Stone.
2-117 Monolithic Mass: Black Sculp-Stone.
2-118 Monolithic Mass: Plaster.
2-119 Monolithic Mass: Pumice Stone.

2—119

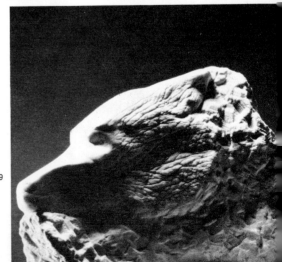

20

121

−122

2-120 Concave-Convex Mass: Detail, Girl's Face.
2-121 Concave-Convex Mass: Driftwood Branch.
2-122 Concave-Convex Mass: Grain Elevators.

Concave-Convex Mass

The intrusion of space by virtue of concavities and convexities occurring in the monolithic mass marks the beginning of a major dematerialization of three-dimensional form. This process was utilized in the Egyptian incised reliefs, took on special importance in the entire field of architecture when it reached its extreme during the Baroque period, and was re-evaluated as a conscious means of sculptural expression in the theory and work of Archipenko at the beginning of the 20th century. Whether by conscious effort or natural occurrence, the interplay of concavities and convexities acting on a three-dimensional form may be found in forms as diverse as the grain elevator, child's face, and driftwood on the opposite page. Thus one does not need a long historical analysis of concave-convex forms to realize their application and to sense their effect on mass. Various forms emphasize either convexities or concavities, as Rudolf Arnheim points out in his book on Art and Visual Perception.

(It is recommended that the reader look over Arnheim's section on "Concavity in Sculpture," pages 193 ff. in Art and Visual Perception, and Alexander Archipenko's chapter on "Concave," pages 51 ff. in Archipenko: Fifty Creative Years, for a more detailed analysis than can be presented in this brief section.)

Two examples of historical importance might serve to represent the convex-oriented work versus the concave-oriented work: the architecture of Francesco Borromini for the former and the sculpture of Alexander Archipenko for the latter. Baroque architecture, to which Borromini was one of the major contributors, was characterized by a tremendous interplay between convex and concave, between forms that thrust outwards and the deep spaces from which they emerged. There was a great sense of interaction, first, between interior and exterior space, and second, between the exterior and the space of the surrounding environment. Two of Borromini's major works in Rome illustrate this with great clarity, San Carlo alle Quattro Fontane (begun 1638, façade 1665-67) and Sant'Ivo (begun 1642). The swelling forms of the façades of both buildings express the concept of an interior space that is pushing outward from inside. The exterior spaces around these buildings are greatly affected by these protuberances. The narrow street that San Carlo faces, with the long, quiet rhythm of the Palazzo Quirinale façade lulling the passer-by into complacency, is quite passive in the area around the church. Suddenly, at the end of the block, the façade of San Carlo thrusts itself outwards, compressing the space and causing considerable visual turbulence in the area. Space seems to lap insistently at the recesses in the façade, but to a much lesser degree than the form pushes outward.

In contrast to Borromini's emphasis on convexity counterpointed by subordinate concavities, we find the contemporary sculptor Archipenko almost exclusively preoccupied with concavity as a new medium of sculptural expression (see Fig. 2-123, page 94). Archipenko was concerned with the concept of space as a material substance and tried to create this feeling for space in his sculpture.

No matter what the emphasis — concavity or convexity — this first stage of dematerialization represents the interaction between a now active space and a monolithic form. Prior to monolithic form one had the feeling that form was the aggressive element forcing its way into a relatively passive space. But once form as a monolith lets its arrogant independence of space be known, space seems to assert itself. Space becomes aggressive. This statement of visual form might be subdivided, as with monolithic mass, into two consecutive conditions. The first condition following monolithic mass might be that in which forms display a predominantly convex quality, implying that space has let itself be known to monolithic form, by a gentle nudge perhaps.

Sensing the intention of the intruding space, the monolithic mass reacts by pushing outwards into the environment at the same time that space is driving inwards. Saliencies appear with their consequent concavities. The more the form thrusts outward, the deeper the concave portions become, until a point is reached where the inward action of space seems to balance the outward thrust of the form. The second condition is thus that in which the monolithic form is penetrated by many concavities. As Arnheim wrote: "Surrounding space, instead of passively consenting to being displaced by the statue, assumes an active role, invades the body, and seizes the contour surfaces of the concave units." (*Art and Visual Perception*, page 194.)

From this point, space will assert itself even more; this assertion will be discussed in the following section.

"In the year 1912, parallel to the modulation of space, I conceived the way to enrich form by introducing significant modulation of the concave. The modulation of the concave, its outlines and whole patterns become an integral part, symbolically as important as the pattern of the elevations." (Archipenko: Fifty Creative Years, page 52.)

"The psychological significance of the concaves in my sculpture derives from creative sources and provokes creative action. They are perceptible as symbols of the absent form. . . .

". . . All positive and negative by the nature of polarity eventually become one. There is no concave without a convex; there is no convex without a concave. Both elements are fused into one significant ensemble. In the creative process, as in life itself, the reality of the negative is a conceptual imprint of the absent positive." (Ibid., page 53.)

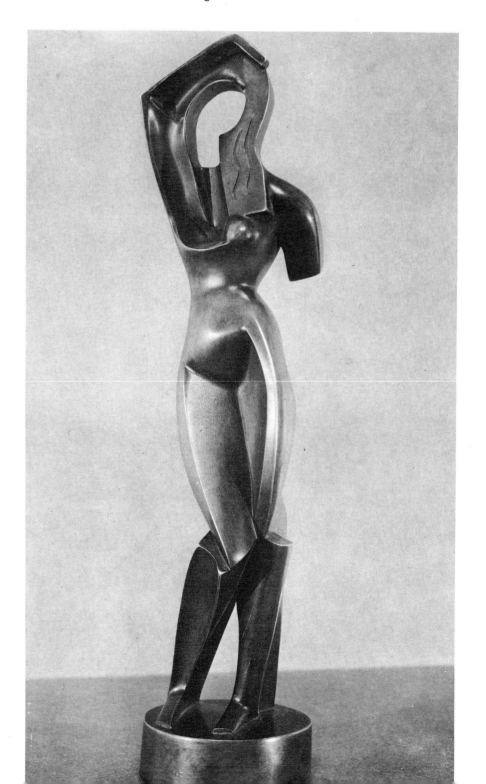

2-123 *Woman Combing her Hair* Alexander Archipenko (1915), (bronze, 13³/₄ inches high). (Collection, Museum of Modern Art, New York. Acquired through the Lillie P. Bliss Bequest.)

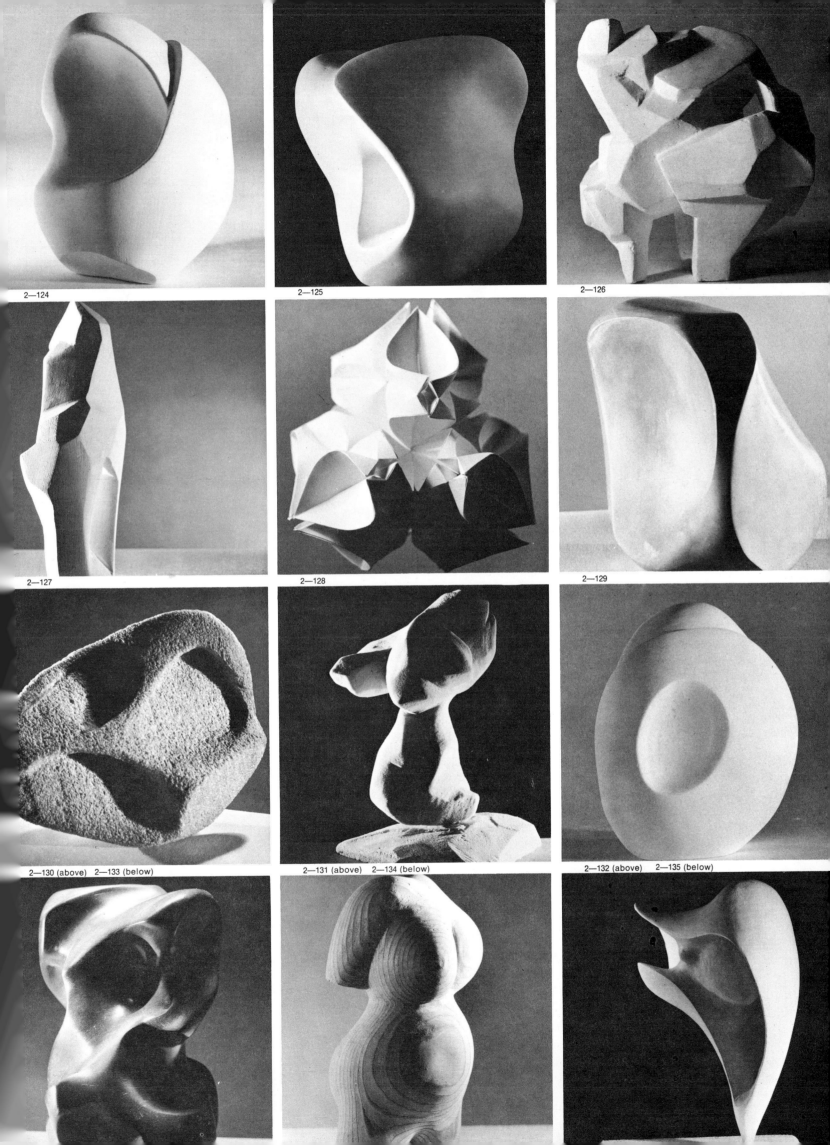

2—124

2—125

2—126

2—127

2—128

2—129

2—130 (above) 2—133 (below)

2—131 (above) 2—134 (below)

2—132 (above) 2—135 (below)

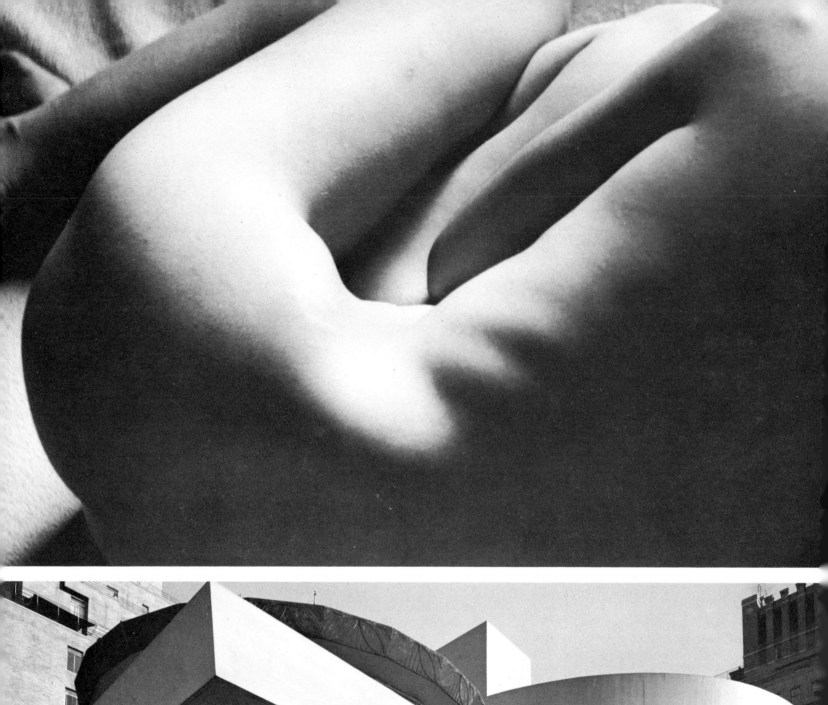

2-136 Penetrated Mass: Sleeping Nude.

2-137 Penetrated Mass: Exterior, The Solomon R. Guggenheim Museum (Frank Lloyd Wright, architect). (Photograph courtesy of The Solomon R. Guggenheim Museum.)

Penetrated Mass

"A piece of stone can have a hole through it and not be weakened — if the hole is of a studied size, shape and direction. On the principle of the arch, it can remain just as strong.
"The first hole made through a piece of stone is a revelation. The hole connects one side to the other, making it immediately more three-dimensional.
"A hole can itself have as much shape-meaning as a solid mass. Sculpture in air is possible, where the stone contains only the hole, which is the intended and considered form.
"The mystery of the hole — the mysterious fascination of caves in hillsides and cliffs." (David Sylvester, *Henry Moore*, page XXXIV.)

Thus wrote Henry Moore, a sculptor who perhaps more than any other has given empty space substance and recognition by means of the penetrated openings in his work (see Fig. 1-139, page 51). In his description we find two different treatments of the problem of the deeply penetrated mass, and these offer a clue to a further subdivision in this portion of the Design Continuum. The first of these, "the mysterious fascination of caves in hillsides and cliffs," describes a condition wherein a three-dimensional mass is broken into by openings of *indeterminate* depth. These openings disappear into darkness, and we are thus borne by the movement and flow of space into the depths of the interior of the form (see illustrations on opposite page). Ulrich Conrads writes about the psychological implications of this type of form in *The Architecture of Fantasy*, page 60:

"There is an attraction in the dark, the impenetrable and the mysterious, in the sense that they cannot be taken in at a glance. Involved is a wish for cozy security and also perhaps a desire to take cover, out of fear. The 'cave' effect need not be restricted to enclosed spaces, but may be just as pronounced on the exterior, where it can arise from a variety of pockets of space."
"A cave as an entity does not let itself be clearly grasped in the sense that a box-like room is easily apprehended and measured at first glance. Rather its charm lies in the indefiniteness of its bounds, in the elusiveness of its volume which evades description, in its shapelessness...." (*Ibid.*, page 13.)

The second division of this form category is one in which the penetration visibly passes through the mass. Space has in a sense achieved a real victory in its interaction with the monolithic mass. It not only acts as an environment for the three-dimensional form but now becomes a physical part of the composition itself. It is an "opening up of volume, the dynamic interpretation of hollows and masses" (Nello Ponente, *Mastroianni,* page 42).

The vast majority of the figurative sculpture of the past — beginning with Greek sculpture as early as the 7th century, B.C., and Roman attempts (see Figs. 1-40 to 1-42, pages 29, 30), then reviving again in the Renaissance and continuing through Maillol into the present — can be characterized by the relation of the solid portions of the figure to open spaces or interstices created by the extended limbs. The sculptors of these periods were obviously conscious of the shape of these spaces and emphasized the openings to a greater or lesser degree, depending upon the tastes of the period and of the individual sculptor.

Similarly, architecture, when it developed to the point of being an art of interior space as well as exterior form (see "The Monument and the Amulet" in *The Art of Sculpture,* by Herbert Read) required openings for the admission of light and human beings. Again, depending upon the period and upon personal taste, these openings went beyond their original function and became a conscious element of architectural expression. Spatial openings set off the massive Greek columns, lent an effect of floating lightness to the dome of the Hagia Sophia, and finally became the dominant visual element in Gothic and in Japanese architecture of the same and following periods. Treatment of full penetration in other periods ranged from the fine courtyard entrances in Renaissance palaces to the more violent interaction of form and space in Baroque architecture. Contemporary architects since Wright have been extremely cognizant of the flow of space into their structures. One might cite Le Corbusier, Kenzo Tange, and Jose Luis Sert among many others whose buildings reveal a great sensitivity to form-space relationships. Le Corbusier was one of the first modern architects to take full advantage of the new technology in construction. He created an architecture that permitted an uninhibited flow of space throughout. His Savoie House expressed this new feeling toward form and space.

"It is impossible to comprehend the Savoie House by a view from a single point; quite literally, it is a construction in space-time. The body of the house has been hollowed out in every direction: from above and below, within and without. A cross section at any point shows inner and outer space penetrating each other inextricably." (Siegfried Giedion, *Space, Time and Architecture,* page 440.)

The reader might also refer to the work of Robert Maillart, who employed thin concrete construction in order to master the interpenetration of form and space in his dramatic bridges.

The interaction of form and space reaches its most intense statement in the deeply penetrated form. Dark pockets of space appear, boring their way relentlessly into the mass, then in their final victory burst through to the other side, creating a new visual condition wherein form and space achieve balance.

Will form regain its monolithic power or will it succumb again to the treacherous intrusions of space? These and other exciting issues will be answered in our next installment. Look for it on the following page.

"Space invades the object, and the object invades space, with the one plastic rhythm." Herbert Read, The Art of Sculpture, *page 113.*

"There is another psychological state in relation to the absent. It can be compared with the musical pause and can be explained as follows: Rhythm in music is possible only if the sound is significantly sequent to the silence, and silence is sequent to sound. Each musical phrase is formed from certain lengths of sound and the length of silences between the sound. Each has its own meaning, as has each word in a phrase. Silence thus speaks. In the Ninth Symphony of Beethoven, a long pause occurs twice and evokes mystery and tension. The use of silence and sound in symphony is analogous to the use of the form of significant space and material in sculpture." Alexander Archipenko, Archipenko: Fifty Creative Years, *page 58.*

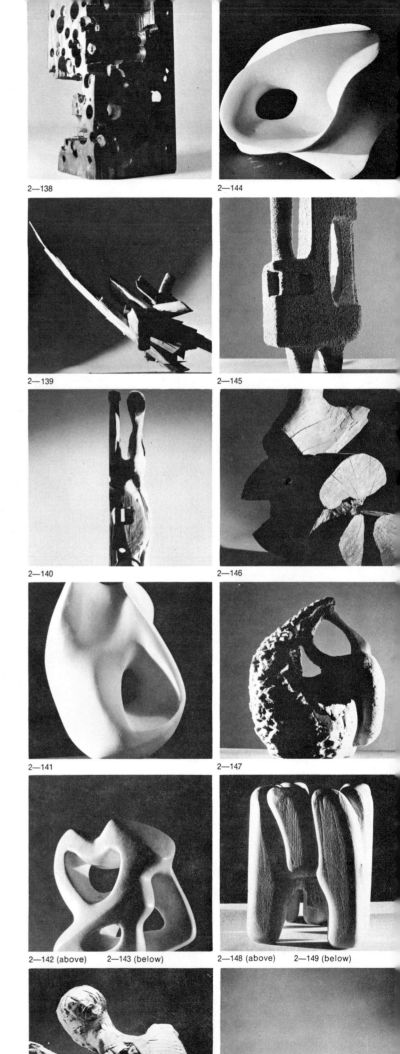

2—138

2—144

2—139

2—145

2—140

2—146

2—141

2—147

2—142 (above)   2—143 (below)

2—148 (above)   2—149 (below)

Student Projects (Figures 2-138 through 2-149)

2-138 Penetrated Mass: Wood.
2-139 Penetrated Mass: Wood.
2-140 Penetrated Mass: Wood.
2-141 Penetrated Mass: Plaster.
2-142 Penetrated Mass: Plaster.
2-143 Penetrated Mass: Papier-Mâché.
2-144 Penetrated Mass: Plaster.
2-145 Penetrated Mass: Sandstone.
2-146 Penetrated Mass: Wood.
2-147 Penetrated Mass: Styrofoam.
2-148 Penetrated Mass: Sculp-Stone.
2-149 Penetrated Mass: Wood.

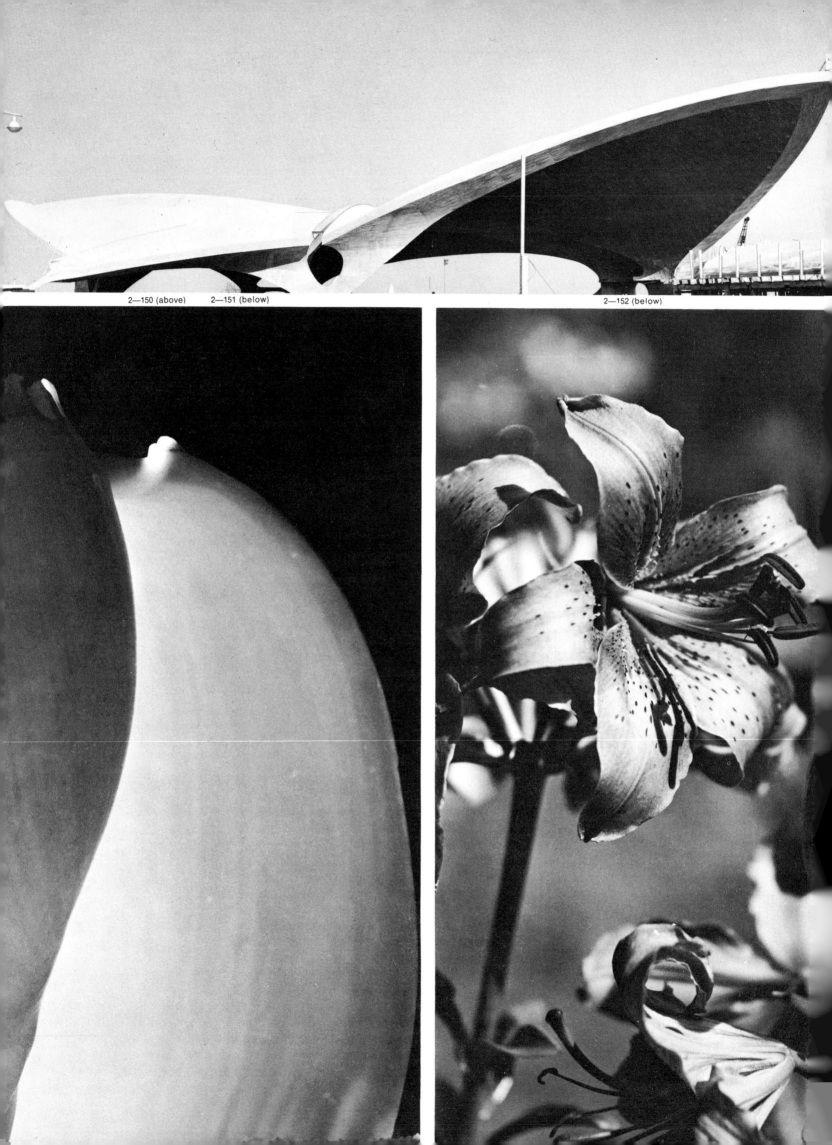

2—150 (above)   2—151 (below)   2—152 (below)

Planar Form

As more and more mass is eroded by the penetration of surrounding space, the three-dimensional object might assume the general characteristics of planar, or shell, forms. These are visual compositions comprised of planes in space (see illustrations on opposite page). The original mass is still suggested by the planes but is now what might be termed a "virtual volume." We create the volume in our perception, whereas in reality the composition is perhaps 75 per cent void. Our eyes move over the surface of the planes and, picking up momentum, jump over the empty areas onto the next plane. Just as our own minds will fill in the remaining portion of a partial line drawing of a circle, we complete the three-dimensional volume. Whether or not this volume appears to be dense or very open clearly depends upon the visual relationship between the planes — their degree of separation, angle of inclination, and the area of the plane itself. For this present study planar forms can be divided into two categories — closed and open. Though both forms are definitely planar in character, they differ in the amount of visual penetration through the form.

Closed planar forms are rather tightly constructed. Though space can flow freely throughout the entire form, our impression of its density is produced by our inability to see through the form (see Fig. 2-151). Whereas physical penetration is considerable, visual penetration is negligible. We can only begin to sense the large percentage of space of which the object is composed.

Open planar forms, on the other hand, are both physically and visually penetrated. Space flows effortlessly into the form, is articulated by the planes, and proceeds outward as easily as it arrived. The observer can see right through most of the object but is still aware of its planar qualities (Fig. 2-150).

There are many areas from which examples of planar forms can be drawn, such as nature, architecture, sculpture, and industrial design. These planar forms have one major characteristic in common in addition to their visual relatedness. They are objects whose structure and consequent form arise from the properties of a three-dimensional plane in space. Curt Seigel, in his comprehensive book on *Structure and Form* (page 179), describes these as "Space Structures" and alludes to both their properties and the various forms that they assume:

"A 'space structure' is one in which the three-dimensionality, inevitably present, is of such importance that it cannot be disregarded without discarding the rational basis of the design. The internal order and outward form of such structures are

2-150 Planar Form: TWA Terminal at Kennedy Airport, New York (Eero Sarinen, architect). (Photograph courtesy of Universal Atlas Cement Division, United States Steel Corporation.)
2-151 Planar Form: Sea Shell.
2-152 Planar Form: Tiger Lilies.

essentially the result of their three-dimensional action. . . . Common utensils have always provided examples of three-dimensional structure. . . . The clay or metal pot, the spoon, the helmet, and the wheel with inclined spokes are ancient, simple forms that work in essentially the same way as a space structure. However, there are even more complicated objects, like forged armor and the wooden canoe, essentially fragile things that owe their considerable strength entirely to their three-dimensional rigidity and testify to man's early technical mastery of the form.

"Today we are surrounded by objects designed on this principle. The self-supporting car body derives its great strength from pressed sheet metal. The same idea is utilized in the design of ships and aircraft. The telephone receiver and the lamp bulb are simply variations on the same theme. Wherever thin sheet or plate is molded into a rigid shape, the inspiration derives from the three-dimensionality of the 'space structure.' "

To extend Seigel's list of planar forms is an easy matter. In nature we find leaves and flower petals (Fig. 2-152, page 100), strips of bark, insect and bird wings, feathers, sea shells (Fig. 2-151), and so on. From architecture one could immediately cite Saarinen's TWA airport terminal (Fig. 2-150, page 100). It was one of the major contemporary attempts to use "free" organic planar form in architecture. Other architects have stayed within the realm of more common mathematical surfaces such as the saddle or combinations of hyperbolic paraboloids in their shell structures.

Certainly the field of sculpture is rich in planar forms. During the Constructivist period sculptors like Gabo, Pevsner, and Moholy-Nagy employed planes to a great degree in their attempts to dematerialize mass into space, light, and movement.

"Pevsner's forms open up and leap into space like projectiles. There is no area of softness or yielding; all is dynamic, structural, and incisive. Under Pevsner's hand the mass disintegrates, weight is shed, and dimensions multiply. Like Gabo, he gives increasing emphasis and vitality to the spatial element. "In his later work, Pevsner's dynamic development in space progressively loses its mechanical character. Within a serried bundle of metal strands, a grand upward movement unfolds in a curved plane. Pevsner's artistic development is akin to that of his brother, Naum Gabo, in his steady approach to organic form. . . . Gabo uses mainly transparent materials, Pevsner prefers bronze, which, disembodied by light, relates the construction to natural atmospheric happenings." (Carola Giedion-Welcker, *Contemporary Sculpture,* page 186).

Both David Smith and Alexander Calder have created many planar works that the reader might investigate. Calder's stabiles, like the one in the series on Modern Sculpture (see Fig. 1-140, page 52), are very fluid and open. One can clearly see the victory of space over form in this work where the planes barely serve to articulate the visual movement of space in and around the form. The extensive works of David Smith, especially his "Voltri" series, offer many fine examples of planar forms, which may be seen in *Voltrone,* by Smith and Carandente. Smith was one of the few sculptors beside Gabo and Pevsner who concentrated their efforts in discovering the sculptural potential and expressive qualities of the plane in space.

2—153
2—154

2—155
2—156

2—157
2—158

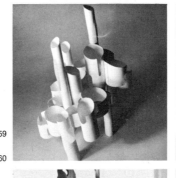

2—159
2—160

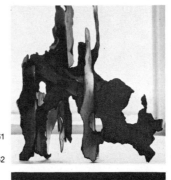

2—161
2—162

2—163
2—164

2—165
2—166

Student Projects *(Figures 2-153 through 2-166)*

2-153 Planar Form: Metal.
2-154 Planar Form: Paper.
2-155 Planar Form: Tin.
2-156 Planar Form: Chrome Automobile Parts.
2-157 Planar Form: Heat-formed Plastic.
2-158 Planar Form: Paper.
2-159 Planar Form: Paper.
2-160 Planar Form: Metal Industrial Parts.
2-161 Planar Form: Wood.
2-162 Planar Form: Paper.
2-163 Planar Form: Heavy Paper.
2-164 Planar Form: Paper.
2-165 Planar Form: Copper and Tin.
2-166 Planar Form: Balsa Wood.

2-167 Planar-Linear Form: Glass House, New Canaan, Connecticut (Philip Johnson, architect). (Photograph, Alexandre Georges.)
2-168 Planar-Linear Form: Cactus.

Planar-Linear Forms

As more and more of the area originally occupied by planes is displaced by space, the total composition assumes a character which could be described as planar-linear. This state could be achieved by two means that may exist separately or in combination. On the one hand, the actual area of the plane might shrink in width, such as the cactus leaves shown in the illustration on the opposite page. The composition then assumes a character that is decidedly linear yet still maintains its planar qualities. The ratio of width to length determines our reaction to an object that is relatively linear. Thus though a plane can still retain its "planeness" if its width is very much narrower than its length, we interpret it as moving toward line.

On the other hand, the total composition may contain elements that are planar-linear in character in conjunction with forms that are still fully planar. Such is the case with the Philip Johnson house, designed by the architect (see the photograph on the opposite page). Both these examples can be termed planar-linear forms. That is, they both retain the characteristics of a transitional state between forms that are completely planar or completely linear. Many of nature's forms, taken in their entirety, are planar-linear forms: a leaf or a flower with its stem; blades of grass; the human hand with its planar palm and linear fingers; or the human skeleton with its planar pelvic bone and linear rib cage. Man-made forms provide endless examples: a frying pan and handle; a shovel, spade, spatula, or any other scraping device; eyeglasses and frames; a belt with its buckle, a window with its panes and framing members, to mention but a few. Architecture and sculpture also offer many planar-linear forms. Japanese architecture with its sliding "shoji" screens are beautiful compositions of planes and line in space. So, too, are many similar contemporary buildings, particularly those designed by Philip Johnson and Mies van der Rohe. Sculptors like Naum Gabo and Reg Butler (see Fig. 1-141, page 52), in addition to working on planes, created many elegant combinations of planes and lines in space.

Gabo experimented with transparent plexiglass planes and lines either scribed directly on the plexiglass or created out of plastic filament that he placed in tension between planes. Through the use of transparency the illusion of dematerialization of mass is further accomplished, for though mass still remains as the structual make-up of the planes, space easily passes through it visually.

> "Constructivism goes further than any of the various tendencies that had preceded it in its insistence on the sublimation of mass into 'virtual volume.' This implies the optical disintegration of material solidity by light so as to enable movement to become a plastic element. (Carola Giedion-Welcker, *Contemporary Sculpture,* page XVI.)

The gaunt figures of one of the most elusive of contemporary sculptors, the late Alberto Giacometti, are reduced to long, thin linear planes in space. For Giacometti the idea of the thin, dematerialized form had existential meaning. Sartre once wrote that Giacometti's figures conveyed to the observer the feeling that he was seeing the figures from a great distance. Giacometti himself writes: "I have never regarded my figures as a compact mass, but as transparent constructions. It was not the outward form of human beings which interested me, but the effect they have had on my inner life." (Carola Giedion-Welcker, *Ibid.,* page 104.)

Thus even in this transitional state several more subtle transitions occur from plane to line in space. Starting with the actual combination of planes and lines, we proceed to forms composed of linearlike planes, such as the cactus. Finally, we can see in the use of transparent materials a further visual reduction of mass into reflections and simultaneous images. In all probability the average person seldom thinks about the remarkable phenomenon of being able to see through solid materials like glass and plastic, yet it is precisely this phenomenon that has had such a staggering effect on our way of life today. When the early Japanese wished to contemplate nature in a view of the outside garden, they had to slide back a translucent panel and open up the entire room to the weather. Although this had decided esthetic and philosophical advantages, its practicability diminished greatly in the winter time, as one might imagine. Contemporary architects, utilizing large expanses of glass, have been able to recapture much of this same intimacy with nature and the visual flow of space from outside to inside while maintaining the functionality of a sealed environment. The architectural forms arising from such use of glass are extremely open in character. In the Johnson house mass is all but disintegrated by the unhampered visual movement of space and the reflections of the environment in the glass. It is a condition in which space is clearly predominant, almost oblivious of the slight articulation that the planar-linear form provides.

"Two major endeavors of modern architecture are fulfilled here, not as unconscious outgrowths of advances in engineering but as the conscious realization of an artist's intent; there is the hovering, vertical grouping of planes which satisfies our feeling for a relational space, and there is the extensive transparency that permits interior and exterior to be seen simultaneously . . . variety of levels of reference, or of points of reference, and simultaneity — the conception of space-time, in short." Siegfried Giedeon, Space, Time and Architecture, page 425.

2—169

2—170

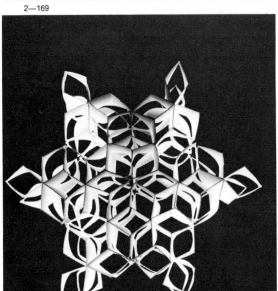

2—171

2—172

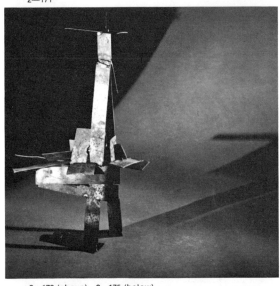

Student Projects *(Figures 2-169 through 2-176)*

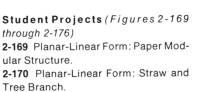

2—173 (above) 2—175 (below)

2—174 (above) 2—176 (below)

2-169 Planar-Linear Form: Paper Modular Structure.

2-170 Planar-Linear Form: Straw and Tree Branch.

2-171 Planar-Linear Form: Paper Modular Composition.

2-172 Planar-Linear Form: Heat-formed Plastic.

2-173 Planar-Linear Form: Tin Sculpture.

2-174 Planar-Linear Form: Ping-Pong Ball and Wire.

2-175 Planar-Linear Form: Glass Sculpture.

2-176 Planar-Linear Form: Balsa Wood.

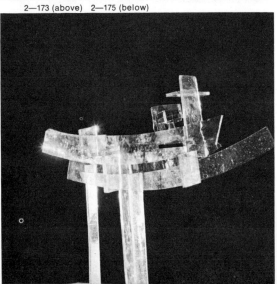

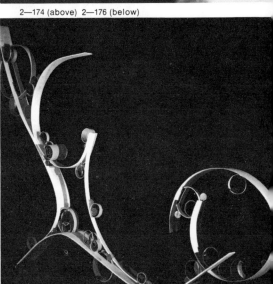

Three-dimensional Linear Form

We have at last reached the final point in the Design Continuum. Having started with line in two-dimensional space, we have passed through various stages in the evolution and dematerialization of form in space and are concluding with line in three-dimensional space. Herbert Read clearly characterizes this last stage in describing the qualities of linear forms in *The Art of Sculpture* (page 114):

"The temptation is to go further than this and to create objects with linear outlines that define space but do not occupy it. At this point, . . . a new art is born: a negative sculpture, a sculpture that denies the basic elements of the art of sculpture as we have hitherto conceived it, a sculpture that rejects all the attributes of palpable mass."

Linear forms are those forms that are comprised entirely of linear elements, such as the group of delicate branches and the steel structural members of the radio tower on the opposite page. These are truly compositions of space, with form serving to articulate but barely participate in the virtual volume perceived by our senses. But there are several further subdivisions that can be discussed as transitional phases in the ultimate disintegration of form in space: These are stable linear structures, mobiles or line in motion and, finally, virtual line in space created by light alone.

Stabile linear structures such as the radio tower, the contemporary

2-177 Line in Space: Tree Branches in Winter.
2-178 Line in Space: Radio Tower.

sculpture in Figure 1-142, page 52, the branches of a tree in winter (illustrated opposite), or telephone lines in the distant horizon create what might be called a fixed virtual volume. The shape of the volume, ambiguous as it may be, never changes in and of itself though we, as observers, may suddenly be aware of changes in its shape in the process of altering our viewing position. The surface of this virtual volume can be conceived of if we imagine a thin film of soap connecting all the outermost points of the structure. Since all these points are fixed, the volume is fixed and only our view of it changes as we move, as with any other stabile work. Those artists and architects who create in this medium are fully aware of the tremendous visual potential of an object which, though physically rigid, shifts in visual form with the slightest movement of the observer. There is not only a sense of the tremendous flow of space in and around the form and of the almost transparent quality of the object, but also of the excitement in a continually and rapidly changing image in time. Giedeon vicariously offers us this experience in his description of the Eiffel Tower in Paris:

"To a previously unknown extent, outer and inner space are interpenetrating. This effect can only be experienced in descending the spiral stairs from the top, when the soaring lines of the structure intersect with the trees, houses, churches, and the serpentine windings of the Seine. The interpenetration of continuously changing viewpoints creates, in the eyes of the moving spectator, a glimpse into four-dimensional experience." (Siegfried Giedion, *Space, Time and Architecture*, page 218.)

There are numerous pieces of industrial architecture similar to the Eiffel Tower. For the connoisseur of more exotic linear architecture, there are the Watts Towers by Simone Rodella (1921-54) in California.

In the field of sculpture the early stabile linear sculptures of Alexander Calder are worthy of investigation. His animal and circus series and heads provide excellent indications of the creative potential of line in a more representational sense. Harry Bertoia and Richard Lippold produced a number of very intricate hanging linear sculptures whose parts are fixed with relation to one another, though in Lippold's case the entire sculpture is free to rotate. The highlights and reflections off the highly polished linear elements in Lippold's sculptures help dissolve the structure into a virtual volume of space and light.

A further dissolution of form occurs in linear objects when one introduces motion into the object itself, such as in mobiles, tree branches, tall rushes, or wheat swaying in the wind. The previously stable virtual volume becomes disjointed; it contracts and expands, shifts and alters its form as the linear compositional elements change position. One senses the dematerialization of mass occurring right before one's eyes. It is as if space is attempting to eliminate that very last bit of form that serves to control it. Moholy-Nagy discusses this type of visual form in his section on the five stages of sculptural development in *Vision in Motion* (page 237). He suggests that mobile sculptures no longer possess the same material characteristics of more solid stable pieces of sculpture and that the added quality of motion imparts to mass a new meaning — as a transmitter of movement.

Calder is without question the major contributor in the area of mobiles. An exhibit of Calder's work held in the Guggenheim Museum in New York in 1964, and which totally filled the entire museum, testified to his virtuosity and prolificness. Other sculptors have taken many directions in the incorporation of motion in their work. Jean Tinguely

2-179 Mobile: *Five Red Arcs*, (ca. 1948) (Sheet metal, metal rods, wire, 47¼ inches high) Alexander Calder. (Photograph courtesy of The Solomon R. Guggenheim Museum.)

"Still, they move in space, and as they move, they define volumes of space. They exist in three-dimensional space just as trees exist in such a space, and they make us conscious of space in much the same way, by waving like branches or trembling like leaves." Herbert Read, The Art of Sculpture, *page 100.*

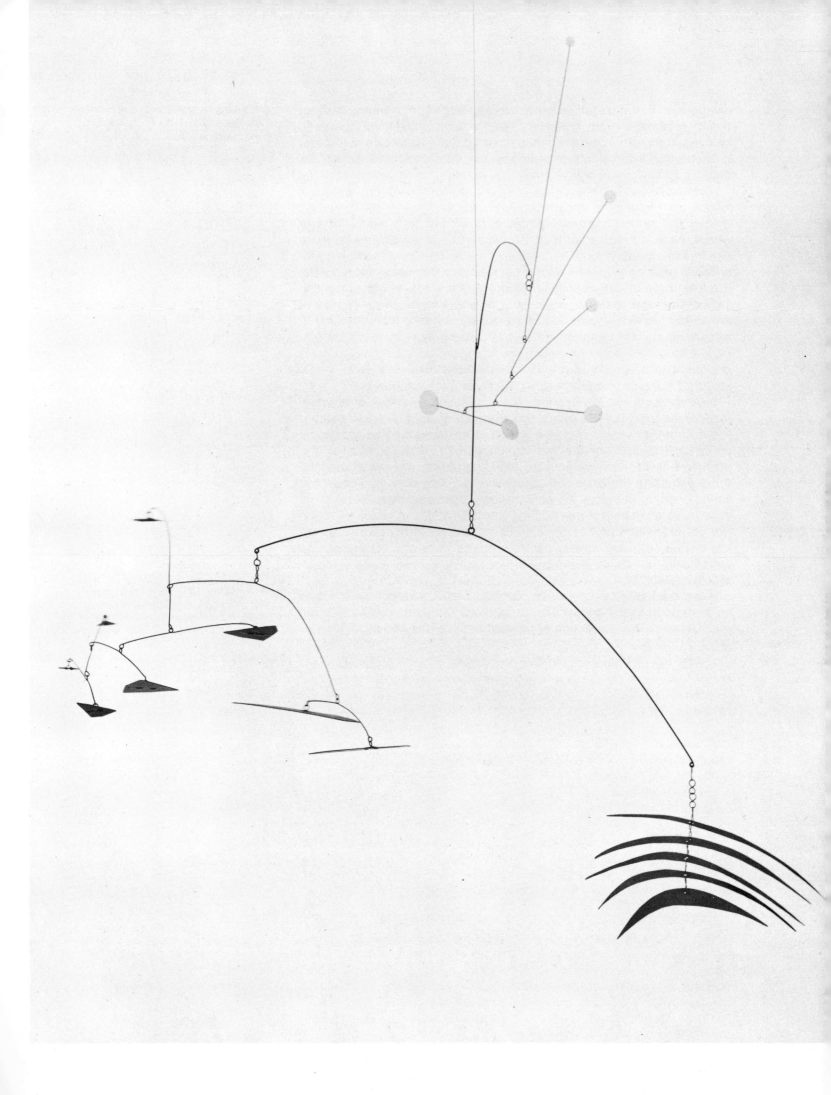

has been one of the leading proponents of adding movement to practically anything — from typewriter mechanisms and bicycle parts to hanging sculpture made of garbage can lids, old fur stoles, and other bits of junk. Calder himself demonstrated that motion can really be applied to any visual form — from flat paintings and reliefs to large sculptures. However, the concern at this point should be limited to motion as it applies to linear sculpture only.

After the mobile there is little place to go but to a visual form in which space is articulated by no physical mass at all. Strangely, there is a readily created form that satisfies these unique conditions. The form will exist permanently on film but for only brief moments in reality. It is the residual virtual volume initiated by the movement of light in space. The most dramatic example of its application is in a display of fireworks — bursting particles of intensely colored light against a blackened sky. One can achieve similar effects by moving a flashlight rapidly in a dark room. Although the light exists in actuality only at one point in time and space, the mind briefly retains a clear visual image of the path that the moving light has just described.

Psychologists and physiologists have proposed a number of possible theories as to why the mind retains the path of light and translates it into a form that we can describe almost as easily as we can a physical entity. One such theory is that the traces of light pass through the mechanisms of the eyes and are then translated into a neurological firing pattern in the brain. An associative process occurs in the mind which creates an image the person might then describe. There is no conclusive evidence of the validity of this theory, but it seems to be one of the few attempts to explain this mysterious formative process in the mind. Interested readers can refer to the work of D. O. Hebb, *The Organization of Behavior,* in which he develops these ideas in much greater detail.

When the light is extinguished nothing is left but darkness — space in its most absolute sense. Form has been vanquished. Space is all that remains. The interaction of form and space has ended.

"Space to be comprehended must be confined." Allen Tucker, Design and the Idea, *page 45.*

". . . the decomposition of the material, destroys all sense of ponderability (sense of mass), all possible appeal to tactile sensibility." Herbert Read, The Art of Sculpture, *page 92.*

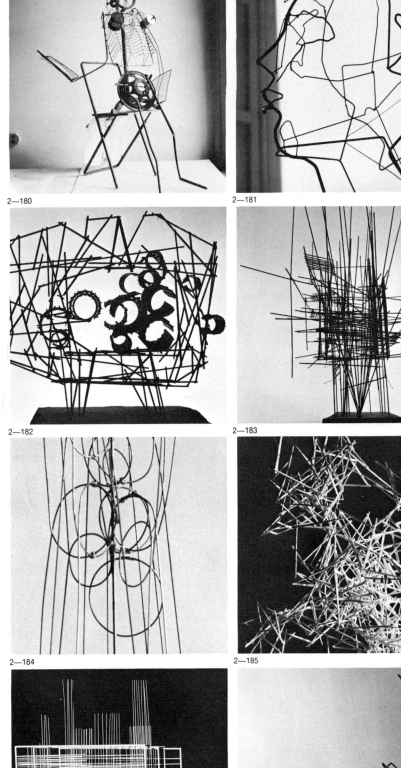

2—180

2—181

2—182

2—183

2—184

2—185

Student Projects *(Figures 2-180 through 2-189)*

2-180 Line in Space: Metal Industrial Parts.

2-181 Line in Space: Wire.

2-182 Line in Space: Balsa Wood and Plastic Hair Rollers.

2-183 Line in Space: Balsa Wood.

2-184 Line in Space: Brass Rod.

2-185 Line in Space: Toothpicks.

2-186 Line in Space: Balsa Wood.

2-187 Line in Space: Metal Rod.

2-188 Mobile: Balsa Wood and Colored Gels.

2-189 Mobile: Wire and Balsa Wood.

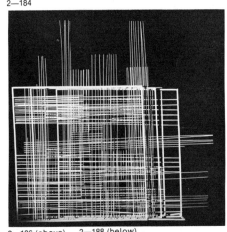

2—186 (above)   2—188 (below)

2—187 (above)   2—189 (below)

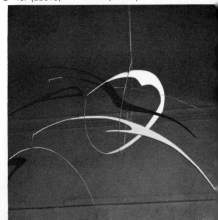

PART III. ORIGINS AND IMPLICATIONS

Origins of the Design Continuum Theory

The origins of the Design Continuum lie, in part, in the works of a number of early revolutionary thinkers in the field of visual form. The influence of these men provided a moral, if not conceptual, basis for this present work. The authors hope that the theory of the Design Continuum will similarly find its way into future studies of visual form in many other areas, for the comprehensiveness of the Design Continuum implies its application to fields as varied as museum exhibits, design instruction, and even the philosophy of art. As a method of organization, the Design Continuum reflects a natural order, that of evolution and dissolution. This conceptual analogy suggests more profound implications, but at the same time clarifies the theory by resolving it into a process which is inherent in life itself.

The Design Continuum approach to the evaluation of visual form offers a departure from established esthetic norms. The traditional approach of art historians has provided us with an invaluable catalogue of man's entire creative output, from prehistory to the forefront of contemporary esthetics. Certainly the contributions of this vast field represent the application of often brilliant and conscientious scholarship to a subject of incredible complexity. The traditional approach of art history has been historically a chronological documentation — one in which national and geographical origins of a work of art serve as the basis for study. During the past 25 to 30 years, a most exciting trend in the study of art forms has begun to emerge which tends to discard somewhat the chronological approach in favor of a stylistic orientation. Among the significant advocates of this trend in esthetics may be cited Henri Focillon (*The Life of Forms in Art*), André Malraux (*The Voices of Silence*), and Laszlo Moholy-Nagy (*The New Vision* and *Vision in Motion*). Their provocative ideas forged a new direction for

3-1 Two-dimensional Linear Composition.

3-2 Line, Shape, and Texture Composition.

The Human Figure *(Figures 3-1 through 3-14)*

An inexhaustible source of sculpture is revealed in the human figure. If we examine the figure selectively, it is not one single form that we see but a vast assemblage of unique and interrelated forms.

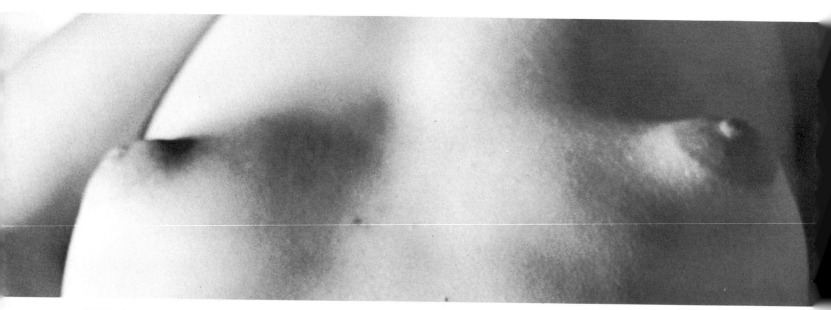

3-7 Environmental Relief with Emerging Ground Forms.

3-10 Concave-Convex Mass.

3-11 Penetrated Mass.

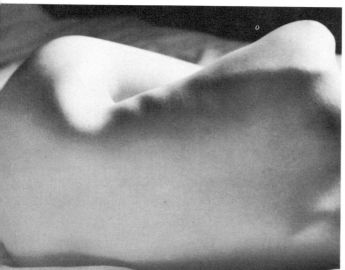

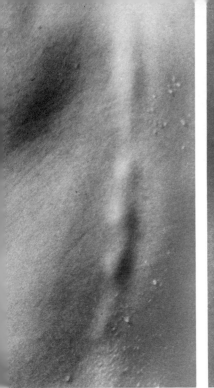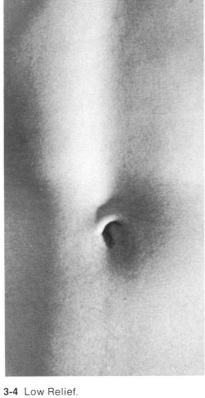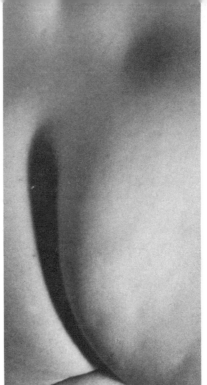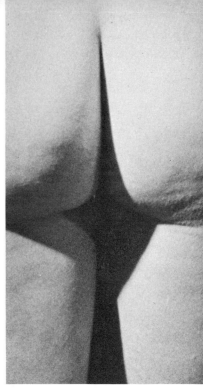

3-3 Very Low Relief.   **3-4** Low Relief.   **3-5** Middle Relief.   **3-6** High Relief.

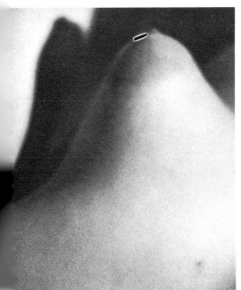

3-8 Sculpture with Base.   **3-9** Monolithic Mass.

3-12 Highly Penetrated Mass.   **3-13** Planar-Linear Form.   **3-14** Lines in Space.

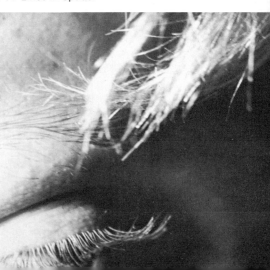

esthetics — one which does not negate the traditional approach of the art historian, but adds to it a further dimension — a stylistic investigation of esthetics irrespective of chronology or country of origin.

Such was the intent of André Malraux. In his classic work, *The Voices of Silence,* Malraux was particularly instrumental in freeing art history and esthetic evaluation from the constricting nature of the chronological approach. The section of this work called "The Imaginary Museum" introduced the concept of comparing stylistic similarities of totally independent cultures, irrespective of their historical context. Once this bold step had been taken, the door was open for comparative systems of evaluation to grow in an independent and healthy climate.

Moholy-Nagy in 1932 and Henri Focillon in 1942 also attempted, in their respective fields of design and art history, to approach the entire study of visual form in a fresh and iconoclastic manner. Both men were very much aware of the insular thinking that predominated in the fields of visual form and design, with a few notable exceptions. Although they expressed their intentions in different ways, each of these men was striving for one primary objective — to speak about forms in art in such a manner that similarities, rather than differences, were stressed. Sometimes their inquiries took the form of very direct statements concerning the interrelationship of the arts, as in Moholy-Nagy's *The New Vision* and *Vision in Motion.* At other times their examination of visual reality contained the subtle implication that there are certain basic forms common to all the arts. The latter proposition can be found in Henri Focillon's *The Life of Forms in Art.* Because of the relationship of Focillon's analysis of form in space to the concept of the Design Continuum, we have chosen to cite the following passage (pages 24 ff.):

> "I should like to attempt this distinction by differentiating between *space as a limit* and *space as an environment.* In the first case, space more or less weighs upon form and rigorously confines its expansion, at the same time that form presses against space as the palm of the hand does upon a table or against a sheet of glass. In the second case, space yields freely to the expansion of volumes which it does not already contain: these move out into space, and there spread forth even as do the forms of light. Space as a limit not only moderates the proliferation of relief, the excesses of projection, the disorder of volumes (which it tends to block into a single mass), but it also strongly affects the modeling. It restrains its undulations and disturbances. . . . But on the other hand, space as an environment, exactly as it delights in the scattering of volumes, in the interplay of voids, in sudden and unexpected perforations, so does it, in the modeling, welcome those multiple, tumbled planes which rend the light asunder. . . . Space as a limit applies likewise to the full-round, over the masses of which it stretches as a skin that guarantees solidity and density. The statue then appears clothed with an even, tranquil light which seems scarcely to move at all across the sober inflections of the form. Inversely, but still within the same order of ideas, space as an environment not only clearly defines a certain way of making statues, but it also affects those reliefs which attempt to express by all manner of devices the semblance of space wherein form moves freely. The baroque state of all styles presents innumerable examples of this. The skin is no longer merely an accurate mural envelope; it is quivering under the

thrust of internal reliefs which seek to come up into space and revel in the light, and which are the evidence of a mass convulsed to its very depths by hidden movements."

From Focillon's imaginative analysis an interaction of form and space can be extracted which is the quintessence of the Design Continuum. The notion of "space as a limit" can be sensed during that part of the Continuum in which form attempts to push its way out into space. All during this evolutionary process, space "restrains" and "moderates" the outward and upward thrusts of form until a condition of rest, balance, or equality is achieved in the monolith. From that point on, space can readily be seen as an active "environment" for form. Whereas space was excluded from the realm of form during the initial portion of the Continuum, space and form begin to merge inextricably in its final stages. Form and space mingle until, finally, form is dissolved into and by the engulfing void. Though the specific details are absent, Focillon's conceptualization of form in space thus foreshadowed the premise of the Design Continuum.

The idea of the dematerialization of form which the latter portion of the Design Continuum describes was employed by a number of people to describe the progression that occurred from Maillol's full roundness to the Cubists, then the Futurists, and finally to the elusive and ephemeral light sculptures of the Constructivists. One of the best examples of this innovation in design thinking can be found in Moholy-Nagy's *Vision in Motion* and *The New Vision*. The author describes five stages of sculptural development: (1) blocked out solid mass; (2) modeled or hollowed form in which some negative penetration takes place; (3) penetrated or bored through block which he calls perforated; (4) suspended sculpture or objects which exist independently of their environment such as a helicopter or a free-floating balloon; and (5) kenetic sculpture such as a mobile in which time and motion are incorporated into the total sculptural form. Thus Moholy-Nagy has provided his reader with an accurate description of form deterioration from solid mass through intrusions of this mass by negative space to a final stage where volume or space is described by moving sculptural forms. These forms possess a minimum of positive mass. We should note however that in the fourth stage the author seems to break premise with the basic progression he has described in the other stages. For example, in stages one, two, three, and five, he deals specifically with the idea of deteriorating mass whereas in stage four, the only conditions he places on the object is that it exist independently from its environment irregardless of how much or how little mass the object contains.

This Moholy-Nagy's description, though less detailed, clearly follows the analysis in the Design Continuum of the deterioration of a solid monolithic mass into planes and then lines into space. Without the revolutionary thinking of such iconoclasts, the study of visual form might not yet have evolved beyond the traditional chronological approach. The premise of the Design Continuum owes a great deal, in conception and direction, to the work of these men.

Applications of the Design Continuum

The comprehensiveness of the Design Continuum permits its application to a number of diverse problems. Of these problems, perhaps the most significant are those of organizing the visual arts into a comprehensible exhibition, of presenting the concept of visual form and space to the subject, and lastly, of reversing the trend toward isolationism within the arts.

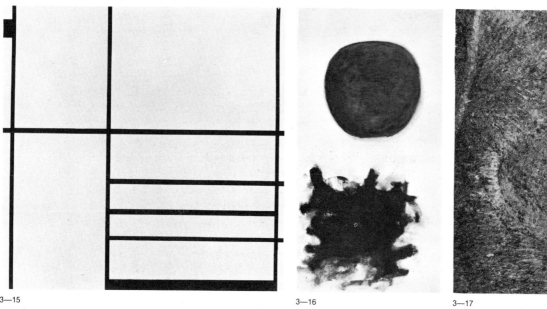

3—15   3—16   3—17

3-15 Line Which Maintains the Integrity of the Surface Plane: Piet Mondrian (1936) *Composition in White, Black and Red* (oil on canvas, 40¹/₂ inches by 41 inches). (Collection, Museum of Modern Art, New York, Gift of the Advisory Committee.)
3-16 Shape and Area with the Beginning of Spatial Illusion: Adolph Gottlieb (1957) *Blast* (oil on canvas, 90¹/₈ inches by 45¹/₈ inches). (Collection, Museum of Modern Art, New York, Philip C. Johnson Fund.)
3-17 Textural Composition with Close Affinity of Figure and Ground Areas: Camille Pissarro (French, 1830-1903) *Bather in the Woods* (oil on canvas, 23³/₄ inches by 28³/₄ inches; signed and dated lower left: C. Pissarro 1867). (The Metropolitan Museum of Art, New York, Bequest of Mrs. H. O. Havemeyer, 1929, The H. O. Havemeyer Collection.)
3-18 Low Relief (Shallow Space): Henri Rousseau (1897) (oil on canvas, 51 inches by 79 inches). (Collection, Musem of Modern Art, New York. Gift of Mrs. Simon Guggenheim.)
3-19 Environmental Sculpture with Strong Suggestion of Emerging Plastic Forms: Workshop of Mantegna, Italian, 15th -16th Century *Madonna and Child with Cherubim* (tempera on wood, 17¹/₂ inches by 11¹/₂ inches). (The Metropolitan Museum of Art, New

Museum Exhibits: Illusory Space *(Figures 3-15 through 3-24)*

For example, the premise of the Design Continuum might be applied to a hypothetical museum visit — one in which visual form is organized according to its "relatedness" rather than to its chronological or national origin. Since this book has dealt so extensively with architecture and sculpture, it might be interesting to organize an exhibit of painting in which the problems of form and space are evaluated with respect to two-dimensional art forms. As was indicated in Part Two, Illusory Space: Painting (pages 60-65), the problem of representing space in a two-dimensional plane has been essentially one of illusion, and the range of solutions in the realm of painting staggers the imagination. Our imaginary exhibit is situated in one large gallery in which ten masterworks are shown comparatively and in a particular sequence. The exhibit is entitled "A Continuum of Illusory Form and Space." As the reader will see on pages 120 and 121, we have reproduced the museum brochure of this exhibit.

The first painting which is encountered is a work by Piet Mondrian, entitled *Composition in White, Black and Red* (Fig. 3-15). The brochure

3—20   3—21

3—18   3—19

York, The Michael Friedsam Collection, 1931.)

3-20 Monolithic Three-dimensional Form: Giovanni Bellini (Venetian, about 1430-1516) *Portrait of a Young Man* (tempera and oil on wood, 14 inches by 11 inches). (The Metropolitan Museum of Art, New York, The Jules S. Bache Collection, 1949.)

3-21 Penetrated Three-dimensional Mass: Jean Auguste Dominique Ingres (French, 1780-1867) *Odalisque en Grisaille* (oil on canvas, 32³/₄ inches by 43 inches). (The Metropolitan Museum of Art, New York, Wolfe Fund, 1938.)

3-22 Three-dimensional Penetrated Masses with Developing Planar Surfaces: Ives Tanguy (1942) *Slowly Toward the North* (oil on canvas, 42 inches by 36 inches). (Collection, Museum of Modern Art, New York, Gift of Philip C. Johnson.)

3-23 Three-dimensional Planar-Linear Form: Joan Miro (1933) *Composition* (oil on canvas, 68¹/₄ inches by 77¹/₄ inches). (Collection, Museum of Modern Art, New York, Gift of the Advisory Committee.)

3-24 Three-dimensional Linear Form: Paul Klee (1922) *Twittering Machine (Zwitscher-Maschine)* (watercolor, pen and ink, 14¹/₄ inches by 12 inches). (Collection, Museum of Modern Art, New York, Purchase.)

caption for this work defines it as an excellent example of the use of line which maintains the integrity of the surface plane. The curator further indicates to the museum visitor that this flat, geometrically abstract painting employs the phenomenon of line and color-space projection. In the second painting in this exhibit, by Adolph Gottlieb, entitled Blast *1* (Fig. 3-16), line has given way to shape and area as a means of accelerating spatial illusion. *Bather in the Woods* (Fig. 3-17), the third painting, by Camille Pissarro, places emphasis on the textural qualities of the oil medium. The entire surface of this work is animated with vigorous brush strokes, in contrast to the Spartan elements of Gottlieb's painting. A closer affinity between figure and ground areas results from the greater emphasis on texture employed by the French artist. The museum curator suggests that the texture quality that we are experiencing in this work is the emergence of illusionistic three-dimensional form, which is carried a step further in the next painting by Henri Rousseau, entitled *The Sleeping Gypsy* (Fig. 3-18). Rousseau's work clearly reveals the qualities of illusionistic low relief. Our curator wishes to remind us by the term "illusionistic" that the purpose of this exhibit is to explore the various contrivances that the painter has

3—22   3—23   3—24

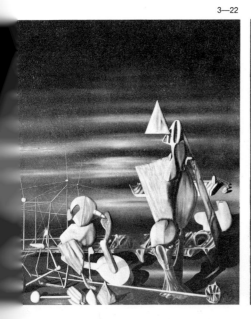

employed historically to simulate the visual conditions that we accept as commonplace in three-dimensional works of sculpture and architecture. He is emphasizing the ingenuity of the painter in creating these effects in the two-dimensional idiom.

The next painting, *Madonna and Child with Cherubim* (Fig. 3-19), by Mantegna, exaggerates the condition of relief that was observed in the Rousseau. Our guide indicates that the Madonna and Child figures in this painting suggest the emergence of a three-dimensional, plastic form. However, these figures are related to their relief-like environment. In the next work, Bellini's *Portrait of a Young Man* (Fig. 3-20), we observe that the plastic form of the young man exists independently in space. Our catalogue designates this condition as the ultimate illusion of monolithic three-dimensional form in painting. The museum curator now indicates to the visitor that from this point on in the gallery tour, the fully plastic form exists independently of its illusionistic three-dimensional space-environment. Ingres' *Odalisque in Grisaille* (Fig. 3-21) takes the monolithic form of Bellini and introduces penetrations such as we see under the sensuous model's arm. The feeling for absolute mass is reduced even by such a subtle intrusion of space through the form. This process is accelerated in Tanguy's *Slowly Toward the North* (Fig. 3-22), wherein large volumes such as we observe in the Ingres have given way to an agglomeration of many smaller forms in a highly penetrated composition. The developing planar qualities of some of the surfaces are also noticeable. Miro's *Composition* (Fig. 3-23) the second to last painting in this exhibit, illustrates a still further dissolution of form. Mass has been reduced to a combination of thin planes and lines that advance and recede in an illusion of infinite space. The last painting, Paul Klee's *Twittering Machine* (Fig. 3-24), is a fitting conclusion to this brief series of paintings. This three-dimensional linear composition recalls Mondrian's two-dimensional work that initiated the exhibit of paintings and, in so doing, concludes this presentation of illusionistic form and space.

It should be clear now that many other exhibits can be arranged following the order of the Design Continuum: for instance, modern and classical sculpture, industrial form, found objects, and so on. Taking another approach, a museum could concentrate on a portion of the Continuum to create an exhibit on a comparison of planar forms as seen in architecture, painting, sculpture, and ancient artifacts, or an exhibit of emerging form in sculpture. In any exhibit created in this manner, the abstract qualities of form, essential for the total understanding of the work, are clearly revealed.

Art School Design Courses

Not only can the premise of the Design Continuum aid the layman in appreciating art through a knowledge and understanding of form, but it also has a potential application as an effective means for organizing a design program in high schools, art schools, and on the college level. Very often in art curriculums today, the study of design is reduced to a series of unrelated two- and three-dimensional "projects." These projects might have considerably more meaning for the student if they were presented in the sequence suggested in Part Two of this work. This does not imply a new pedagogy or an arbitrary imposition of dogma on the teaching techniques and premises of design instructors. It is quite likely that most curriculum of basic design study today already deal with many of the areas suggested by the Design Continuum. However, the various form classifications in the Design Continuum provide a basis for what would be a more compre-

". . . for design needs to be seen from the outset as an organic whole, not as a series of unrelated compartments. One of the most important characteristics of the structure of design is wholeness — continuity. The notion of continuity, of closely related sequences, is fundamental not only to what we produce in design but to our methods for producing it." Norman Newton, An Approach to Design, page 82.

hensive and structural design course one to two years in duration. The usual emphasis on two-dimensional media found in beginning courses at most schools correlates quite logically with the beginning stages of the Design Continuum. Similarly, three-dimensional design, which is often a completely separate subject of study, is dealt with in the latter portion of the Design Continuum. With the inclusion of problems in the areas of *textured surfaces, relief, environmental relief, environmental sculpture,* and *sculpture with base,* three-dimensional design is treated as a logical extension of two-dimensional design — the whole being seen as a coherent sequence of ideas.

The concept of the Design Continuum could create a sequence for the presentation of design problems. The content of each problem would be dependent solely upon the interest, background, and goals of the individual instructor. Thus in a school of architecture the problems could be approached from an architectonic point of view. An instructor who normally utilizes the forms of nature as a point of departure could clearly structure a course along these lines. An instructor with a strong background in fine arts could readily incorporate classical and modern art forms as illustrations. Individual problems could be as varied as the design for a children's playground or an assemblage in *environmental relief,* the sculpting of a strongly monolithic head or the design for a refrigerator in *monolithic* form, the design for a kite or an architectural shell structure in *planar* forms. The variety of problem assignments in each of the categories of the Design Continuum should challenge the imagination of any design instructor.

For those schools equipped with even modest still camera or motion picture equipment, this concept could be illustrated in a particularly convincing fashion through the use of the cinematographer's method. The selective eye of the camera has the singular advantage of isolating a particular form from the confusion of its environment. This act of selecting a form and studying its essential character is fundamental to the development of greater sensitivity in a student. The technical demands of the motion picture medium are assets in the learning process. For instance, before the student can utilize lighting techniques to project a three-dimensional form successfully on film, he must make a thoughtful and serious analysis of that form. The art of film editing allows the student to create simultaneous viewing of two related objects. This time-space juxtaposition is unique to the film medium. Cutting, fades, cross dissolves, flashback scenes, and other editing techniques also enable the film-maker to illustrate the comparative premises of the Design Continuum method.

Cross-Discipline Communication

A third and perhaps the most far-reaching potential of the Design Continuum is its capacity to help reverse the trend toward parochialism among painters, sculptors, architects, and artisans today. It is almost the fashion for painters to ridicule the "commercialism" of the architect and the designer; in retaliation the architect, sensing that his craft is central to the very existence of society, looks with disdain on the "irresponsible dabblings" of the painter. To some degree the sculptor, hampered by the scale and actual physical weight of his creations, enjoys neither the freedom of the painter nor the sense of achievement of the architect. And finally, the artisan, whose craft often involves skills equal to those associated with the fine arts, is normally treated condescendingly because his work involves materials and processes that are not part of the fine arts tradition. Though their means of expression vary greatly, the crafts as well as the fine arts

3—25

deal with the problem of form and can be readily.compared on this basis. But to do so requires a common language that defines their relatedness in the area of form. Perhaps the Design Continuum can provide the genesis of such a language. This interrelationship of the arts to one another and to the social forces that mold them is imperative in our highly complex metropolitan societies today, for isolation can only weaken the influence that the arts extend to contemporary culture. Arnold Hauser in his brilliant work, *The Social History of Art,* documented the interrelationship of the arts as did Moholy-Nagy and Focillon. Perhaps this study, too, can help to suggest a common frame of reference among the fiercely independent protagonists of today's esthetic discipline.

3—26

Natural Order

The Design Continuum viewed in its entirety reveals a peculiar process which deserves specific mention. The concern of the first half of the continuum demonstrates the build-up, emergence, and coalescence of form from a condition of absolute flatness, through the gradual articulation of a surface in space, to a final complete break with its form environment in a monolithic state. It is an evolutionary process — one of growth, materialization, formation. Form seems to be pushing its way out into a restricting, limiting space. The second half of the Continuum is quite the opposite. Though the object is always in a three-dimensional state, the second half traces the dematerialization of the form. The solidity of the monolith is dissolved by space — first by concavities and convexities, then holes, and finally reduces to planes and lines. One thinks of erosion, decay, or dissolution. The entire Continuum may be seen as the growth or evolution of form followed by its dematerialization or dissolution by space — evolution and dissolution, growth and decay.

3—27

3—28

The obvious analogy to this process of organization is that of nature's own methods — a period of development followed by one of decline. It is the story of mountains pushed from the sea only to be eroded by rain, rivers, and glaciers. But it is also the story of empires, which like Rome rise to grandeur — only to sink into decay. It is the rose that emerges from its monolithic bud into the full flowering of its plane-like petals — only to disintegrate into nothingness. It is human life — from birth and childhood, through adulthood and old age, to death. Though it was not intended as such, this organization of visual form can be clearly seen as reflecting the natural order of life. It somehow adds another validation to man's concept of nature and its relation to art. Western works like Blossfeldt's *Art Forms in Nature* and Kepes's *New Landscape* reveal nature and natural phenomena as a vast source of varying abstract forms and patterns that can enrich the visual vocabulary of any artist. The Oriental philosophies, on the other hand, are much more concerned with the *relationship* between all natural things than with the isolated, static fact by itself. Zen philosophy deals with the idea of growth and change as the essence of life and nature and demonstrates how this feature may be isolated and incorporated into the creations of man. The partially empty page and the rock arrangement both suggest growth and movement toward completion. The relationship between positive mass and negative space in Japanese gardens, room interiors, screen paintings, and flower arrangement is dynamic and requires that the observer participate actively in the total visual experience. The experience is not complete until object and observer become one, and even then, since

3—29

3—30

3—31

3—32

3—33

"Moreover, the separation of architecture . . . from arts such as painting and sculpture makes a mess of the historical development of the arts...." John Dewey, Art as Experience, *page 222.*

"Man's spirit is truly free in the impregnability of a high intellectual self-expression. The power of formal order alone authorizes the ease and spontaneity of creation." Henri Focillon, The Life of Forms in Art, *page 14.*

growth and change in time are inherent in man's life, the experience is never a static one. Thus to the Oriental the essential natural qualities of growth and change play a profound role, not only in the creation of works of art but also in the understanding of them. The authors do not pretend that the relationship of the Design Continuum theory to nature is of the same profundity or sophistication as the Oriental philosophy. However, the growth and decay process of nature provides a remarkably clear and logical metaphor by which to organize visual form. The analogy is apparent. Its significance is up to the reader to ascertain.

Order is thus fundamental to nature and to man, since he is part of nature. The alternation of day and night, the four seasons, the rotation of the planets and stars, natural symmetry, and the order of life itself provide models for man to assess and follow. Man needs order to comprehend his activities. He tries to create an orderly society, to order his life, to order the events of history, to order science, to establish a theory of logic as in the field of mathematics, to run business ventures. Bus and train schedules, lunch breaks and dinner time, the calendar and the clock — all help to create a sense of order. If he feels order to be so important and essential to daily life, it is odd that man has not sought to order the visual world of forms around him in a purely abstract sense. When one looks for order in the field of art as a whole, the major emphasis appears to be on historical style. Thus museums categorize the Egyptian age, Byzantine age, Greek period, Gothic, and so forth. That man feels the need for an order of position can be seen in the arrangement of rooms, cupboards, convention halls, typical street plans, and town layouts. Man wants to know where things are or have come from. Thus we are told from what country or city a work of art comes, and this helps us to build a picture of the culture of that particular area.

But what about an order of form and space? It becomes even more critical now to develop a sense of order for visual form and space in view of the considerable number of highly abstract art and architectural works of recent years. Seen apart or in combination, they soon numb the emotional response of the viewer. They begin to "all look alike," because the eye and mind have not yet been given the needed tools of visual evaluation to begin to order form. It is hoped that the Design Continuum will begin to provide the reader, no matter what his occupation or intentions, with this basis. At the same time the authors insist that these methods do not operate to the exclusion of other ways of looking at form. Used in combination with art history, nature studies like biology or zoology, psychology or perception, or any other subject areas dealing with form, the Design Continuum provides an orderly overview of the entire spectrum of visual form.

Conclusion

In *The Life of Forms in Art,* Henri Focillon cautions about subjecting form to an analysis such as that of the Design Continuum. He warns of its deceptive orderliness, its single-minded directness, its use of forced transitions where there is discord and, finally, its inability to make room for the revolutionary energy of inventors. The authors are the first to admit the presence of the first three, if in fact they are issues.

First, placing visual form in a sequence of categories creates a sense of order out of the complete disarray and disorder around us. It is true that transitions of this type may be seen in all growth and decay patterns in nature, but this simply provides an interesting analogy and suggests a certain logic in the categories. The authors do not intend by this logic to deceive anyone into thinking that all is really order, or that nature or man always creates with this order in mind. The purpose of establishing such an order is only to provide a framework for an objective analysis of all visual forms which will help to clarify them by type.

Second, the apparent single-minded directness of such an order, although purposely direct in its presentation, actually resulted from a deductive procedure that considered an entire spectrum of potential categories. Furthermore, the authors have insisted that the Design Continuum be emphasized in conjunction with, rather than to the exclusion of, other methods for studying visual form.

Third, where sharp breaks occurred in the early planning of the Design Continuum the authors strongly felt the need for creating transitional forms such as environmental relief, environmental sculpture, sculpture with base, and planar-linear forms. Admittedly some of these categories were conceived in relation to only one particular type of natural or man-made form. For example, the environmental relief, which seemed to be a logical extension of high relief, was originally limited to site planning and architecture. To create this classification with its evidence in just one field would have been a tenuous assumption, since the object of the Design Continuum is to explain and relate visual forms in all fields. Later, however, the expression of environmental relief became apparent in sculpture, sculpto-paintings, nature, and many other areas. The other transitional forms were substantiated in like manner.

The fourth warning that Focillon gives is one of deepest concern to the authors. He warns of the inability of any theory to allow for inventions that might fall outside the bounds of the theory. In the case of the Design Continuum, there might be natural or artistic creations that combine (as many do) a number of categories. For example, the Guggenheim Museum (Fig. 2-136) is a fine example of a penetrated form, with its strong conjoined masses permitting space to flow around them. But if we isolate the form in the upper left, we find it to be very monolithic, whereas the large right-hand mass still preserves a sense of penetration. Coming in closer, we can notice the texture of the concrete surface. Or perhaps we can study the gallery of the building (the inverted cone form) in its relation to the rest of the building as an example of a sculpture with a base. The building in its entirety relates to the rest of the cityscape as a ground form. And if we take an airplane high enough over the city it becomes part of a giant relief below us. Thus one building is, in reality, a composite of visual forms; which is predominant depends upon the viewer's frame of reference. A composite form does not break premise with the organization of the Design Continuum, because the Continuum is not a theory of absolutes but deals with a constantly shifting objective visual reality.

But what of forms that are distinct from the categories presented and do not permit clear analysis? Though we do not know what they may be, we can offer but one comment toward their understanding. The Design Continuum is planned to include the overwhelming majority of visual forms that the viewer will experience. If in the process of looking at the world the viewer discovers a form which does not fit, he has truly begun to exercise the type of decision-making and analysis of visual form the absence of which prompted the writing of this book. The authors would encourage the reader to try to discover these additional forms in sculpture, architecture, painting, nature, and industrial design. In so doing he will begin to discover, categorize, and, hopefully, clarify the incredibly diverse character of our visual environment.

"Through its culture, plastic art shows a growth toward the culmination of limited form, then a dissolution of this form and a determination of the freed constructive elements (planes, colors, lines). If we observe this fact, we can conclude that our whole culture equally reveals the same process." Piet Mondrian, Plastic Art and Pure Plastic Art, *page 39.*

". . . and the artist who pauses to try to understand his own activities cannot remain content to regard them as 'purely aesthetic.' He must wonder why they seem to him so intensely important, and yet are so neglected and misunderstood by science, and by society. The divergence of the two attitudes can only be validly overcome in one way: by a broadened understanding of the importance of form in all realms, not only in the external world but also in the unconscious roots of all human activities. Indeed we may discover that there is nothing wholly formless in nature, that if there were it could never be known to man, and that every particular form has its own special significance within the universal order of which man is part." Lancelot Whyte, Aspects of Form, *page 4.*

"Above all things, sculpture must be informed by a quality of integration sufficient to sustain the belief that its forms arise, as it were, like those of nature, from some profound inward necessity and that they, too, exist in the absolute unity and independence of their being, by reason of their obedience to certain analogous laws." E. H. Ramsden, Sculpture: Theme and Variations, *page 12.*

"Elevating in its joyousness, far beyond the aesthetic sensation, is the recognition that the hidden creative forces, to the fluctuations of which we, as beings created by Nature, are subject, are ruling everywhere with the same impartiality and authority in the works produced by each generation as a type of its existence, as well as in the most perishable and most delicate creations of Nature." Karl Blossfeldt, Art Forms in Nature, *page X.*

PART IV. COLOR SECTION

In this section student works, natural forms, and man-made objects are illustrated in a manner that expresses the concept of the Design Continuum in greater detail. It is the most complex presentation in this book for it operates in two directions simultaneously. Each horizontal row illustrates a continuum. The top row shows projects created by students in a university-level design course. The middle row shows forms found in nature. The bottom row shows man-made objects selected because in most instances they are found art, in contrast to the deliberate creations of the artist. It is suggested that the reader view each series horizontally, independent of the other two. In this manner full attention can be given to the transitions between each successive stage of the Continuum. Once the reader becomes familiar with each series he should proceed to study the vertical columns on each page. There he will find three objects that represent the same stage in the Continuum: the vertical direction depicts identical form relationships while the horizontal direction explores sequential form development.

By viewing both directions simultaneously the reader will sense both the unity and diversity of form. He should bear in mind that each of the three continuums illustrated simultaneously contain 24 stages, and that only three steps are shown on each page. The concept that the authors are attempting to explain in this eight-page section would be clearer to the reader if, ideally, all eight pages could be extended edge to edge so that the entire 24 steps could be seen in one sweep of the eye. Unfortunately the limitations of book format prevent such a display; it is to be hoped, however, that the reader will familiarize himself with the entire scope of this concept by following each step of the development of the student, nature and man-made object continuums throughout the color section.

It might prove to be of some interest to the reader to refer back to other continuums which appear in visual form in other parts of this book. The Classical Sculpture Series on pages 26-30 or the Modern Sculpture Series on pages 48-52 might be compared to the Student Series in the top row of this section; the Shell Series on page 46, the Human Figure Series on page 116-117, or the Flower Series on page 124 might be compared to the Nature Continuum in the center row of this section; and finally, the Kitchen Utensils Series on pages 24-25 or the Mexican Folk Art Series on pages 44-45 might be compared to the Man-made Objects Continuum which appears on the bottom row of this section. Such a perusal and review of these visualizations of the design continuum should help to crystallize this concept for the reader.

Color Photographs (*pages 129-136*):

129

Step One: In this stage of the continuum, only line on a two-dimensional surface is apparent. This first trio depicts the most spartan elements of design, namely, line on a flat surface with no other embellishment.
1A. Student Project: Two-dimensional Linear Composition (ink on paper).
1B. Nature: Linear Grain Patterns in a Pebble.
1C. Man-made Object: Signatures on the *Declaration of Independence.*

Step Two: With the introduction of value and color contrasts in this second trio, the illusion of space begins to emerge in spite of the essentially flat surface upon which the shapes are described. Notice how the aerial photograph, the sign, and the striped student-design read as describing the same degree of spatial illusion.
2A. Student Project: Line and Shape in a Two-dimensional Space (watercolor on cardboard).
2B. Nature: Aerial View of Farmlands near Syracuse, New York.
2C. Man-Made Object: Detail of Weathered Sign.

Step Three: Notice in this third trio of photographs how the illusion of space is heightened through the introduction of the element of texture and a higher chroma color. This phenomena is particularly noticeable in the top photograph where the hot red-orange and the bright blue-greens wage their relentless war for spatial dominance.
3A. Student Project: Illusory Space Created by the Juxtaposition of Complementary Colors (colored paper).
3B. Nature: Leaf of a Tropical Plant.
3C. Man-Made Object: Detail of Fabric Design.

130

Step Four: Here we witness the introduction of actual physical relief for the first time in this continuum. We must bear in mind that scale of relief is solely dependent on the frame of reference of the observer; note in this trio that the student collage appears to have about the same amount of relief projection as the shell or the farmhouse door in spite of the obvious differences in scale. This apparent discrepancy is explained when we realize that the distance from the observer's eye to the object is the controlling factor in all human perception of form.
4A. Student Project: Collage of Textured Surfaces (paper, cardboard, and sandpaper).
4B. Nature: Detail of a Scallop Shell.
4C. Man-Made Object: Detail of Farmhouse Door.

Step Five: The textural emphasis in this trio of low reliefs should be the significant consideration for the observer.
5A. Student Project: Textured Surface (glue, rubber cement, and pastel on matboard).
5B. Nature: Interior of Abalone Shell.
5C. Man-Made Object: Household Sponge.

Step Six: In this stage of the continuum, physical projection of form up into the environmental space is apparent. As the relief-like surface is described we begin to see the introduction of light and shadow as a new and important factor; line, shape, and texture are joined as form emerges into the space of the third dimension.
6A. Student Project: Low Relief (fiberboard).
6B. Nature: Eroded Wood Form.
6C. Man-Made Object: Detail of Danish Carved Wood Tobacco Box.

131

Step Seven: In this trio of middle reliefs, the element of light and shadow serves to describe the greater penetration into the environmental space which these objects have achieved.
7A. Student Project: Middle Relief (plaster).
7B. Nature: California Pine Cone.
7C. Man-Made Object: Drawers from Treadle Sewing Machine.

Step Eight: Steep projections and deep undercutting characterize this group of high reliefs and yet the forms still read as interconnected one to the other. This is last stage of the pure relief form in this continuum; we will notice in step nine that small environmental and essentially independent ground forms will begin to emerge. This subtle but tremendously important change in form marks the beginning of the fully three-dimensional and independent sculptural form.
8A. Student Project: High Relief (plaster).
8B. Nature: Gouged Wood Form.
8C. Man-Made Object: Time Clock, circa 1910.

Step Nine: Notice how the viewing angle of the observer has been shifted in this trio of environmental reliefs with ground-forms. Instead of the frontal view which was employed in steps 1-8, we now look down on these forms so that their three-dimensional character can be studied with greater accuracy. We are still confronted with a predominantly relief-like surface; however, we notice that small objects such as a piece of prominent charcoal, a spool of thread, or a cork dome, project up into space independent of the relief surface. Such a form can be designated as a "ground form".
9A. Student Project: Environmental Relief with Low Ground Forms (cork).
9B. Nature: Charcoal Fire.
9C. Man-Made Object: Assemblage of Sewing Materials.

132

Step Ten: In step ten of this continuum, the ground forms are already taking on a more prominent role. The environmental relief is still the dominant factor in the composition and the ground forms are clearly subordinate in nature. The horizontal relief surface sets the tone and defines the basic character of these emerging forms.
10A. Student Project: Environmental Relief with Accentuated Ground Forms (painted clay).
10B. Nature: Conch Shell.
10C. Man-Made Object: Scandinavian Folk Toy.

Step Eleven: Here we are still dealing with a relief surface, but now the ground-forms are coalescing into singular and more prominent vertical forms. We also notice, in the top two frames of this trio particularly, that the ground-forms take their essential character and structure from the nature of the relief environment. If the relief surface is penetrated, as we observe in figure 11A, then the ground-form itself is also penetrated; if the surface is modular and planar as is apparent in figure 11B, then the essential character of the emerging ground-form will derive from this dominant relief surface.
11A. Student Project: Environmental Relief with Strong Ground Forms (plaster).
11B. Nature: Zinnia.
11C. Man-Made Object: Muffin Tin.

Step Twelve: In this stage, the ground-form has taken on such an insistent character of its own that it can be more accurately described as an environmental sculpture.
12A. Student Project: Environmental Sculpture (wood).
12B. Nature: Bole on a Tree Trunk.
12C. Man-Made Object: Antique Carpenter's Plane.

(Captions continued on page 137)

1A

2A

3A

1B (above) • 1C (below)

2B (above) • 2C (below)

3B (above) • 3C (below)

4A

5A

6A

4B (above) • 4C (below)

5B (above) • 5C (below)

6B (above) • 6C (below)

7A

8A

9A

7B (above) • 7C (below)

8B (above) • 8C (below)

9B (above) • 9C (below)

10A

11A

12A

10B (above) • 10C (below)

11B (above) • 11C (below)

12B (above) • 12C (below)

13A

14A

15A

13B (above) • 13C (below)

14B (above) • 14C (below)

15B (above) • 15C (below)

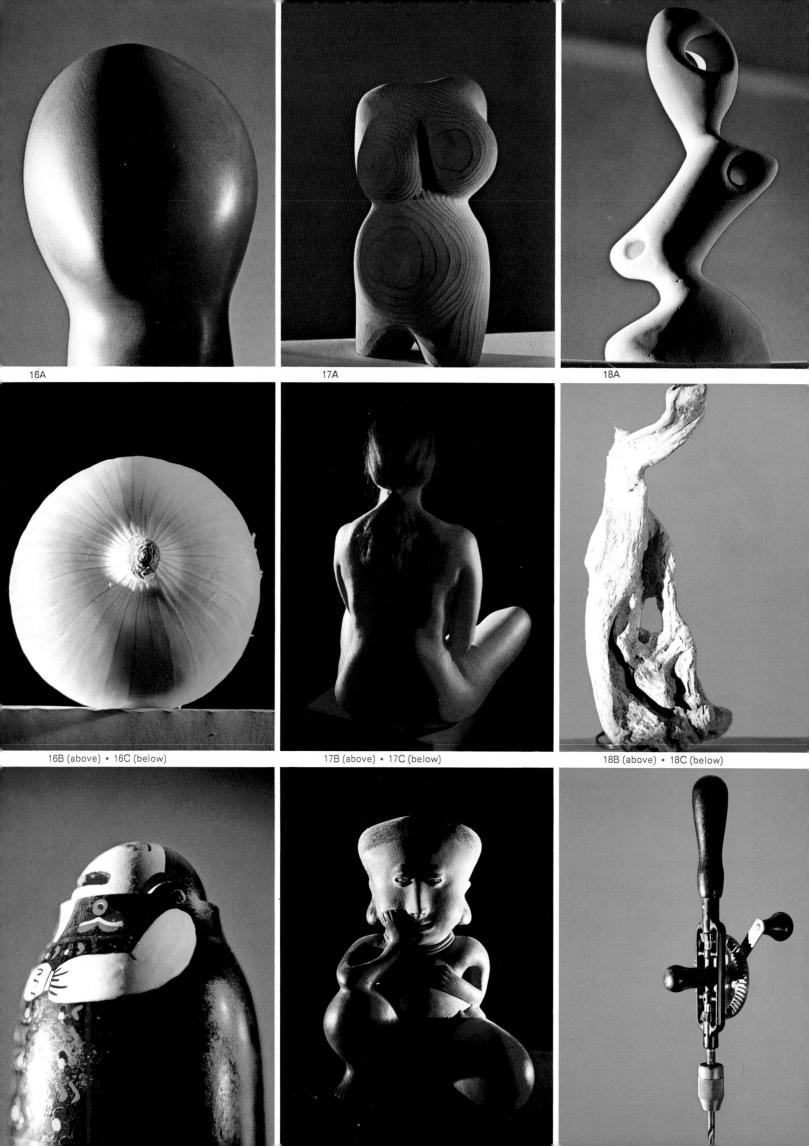

16A

17A

18A

16B (above) • 16C (below)

17B (above) • 17C (below)

18B (above) • 18C (below)

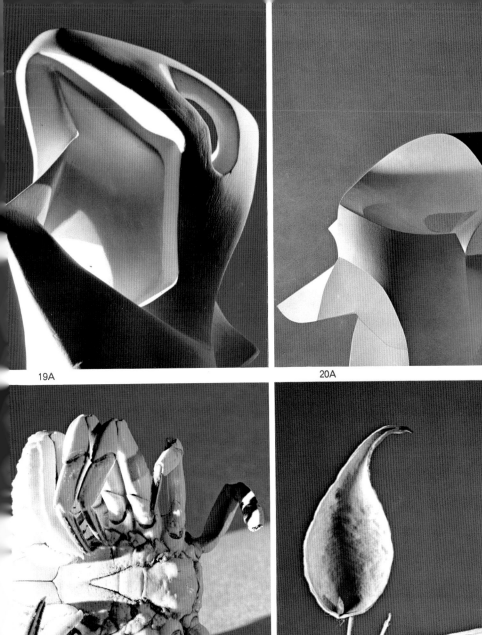

19A

20A

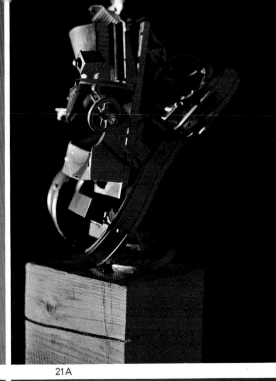

21A

19B (above) • 19C (below)

20B (above) • 20C (below)

21B (above) • 21C (below)

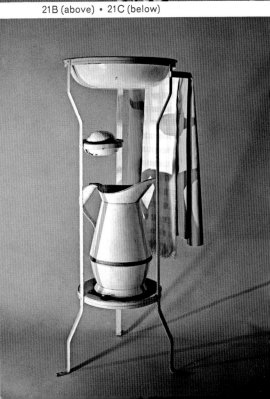

22A

23A

24A

22B (above) • 22C (below)

23B (above) • 23C (below)

24B (above) • 24C (below)

(Captions continued)

Step Thirteen: With this trio of sculptural compositions, the handle of a banjo, a protruberance of shell forms, or a massive plaster shape, while still subordinate to a broad and still dominant base, one can clearly observe the independent character of the three-dimensional sculpture.
13A. Student Project: Sculpture with Predominant Base (plaster).
13B. Nature: Murex Shell.
13C. Man-Made Object: Antique Banjo-Uke.

Step Fourteen: An equilibrium between the mass of the base and the opposing force of the vertical sculpture is achieved in this trio of compositions. It should be noted that in each case, the sculpture reflects certain fundamental characteristics of its base. We can also observe that the vantage point of the observer is lowering throughout the environmental stage so that the form of the three-dimensional sculpture can be revealed.
14A. Student Project: Sculpture with Base of Balanced Emphasis (plaster).
14B. Nature: Woman's Ear.
14C. Man-Made Object: Lemon Juicer.

Step Fifteen: The last vestige of the sculptural base is disappearing in this phase of the continuum; notice how the sculptural form anticipates the full monolith of the next stage of this continuum.
15A. Student Project: Sculpture with Minimal Base (white soapstone).
15B. Nature: Butternut Squash.
15C. Man-Made Object: Antique Wood Pestle.

133

Step Sixteen: Here we observe the triumph of three-dimensional positive mass; form in its most positive state repels any intrusions of negative space. The base as an element of sculpture has disappeared; all that remains is pure mass.
16A. Student Project: Monolithic Mass (black soapstone).
16B. Nature: Onion.
16C. Man-Made Object: Norwegian Child's Bank.

Step Seventeen: The triumph of pure form is short lived. No sooner has it freed itself from the constraints of the encumbering base than it must now begin to surrender its surface to the intrusions of an unrelenting negative space. In all three examples under consideration, a still solid mass has already undergone a significant erosion. This phase of surface eruption recalls the relief transitions already encountered in steps 6-12 of this continuum. Now, however, we are dealing with the transformation of a full three-dimensional form, whereas in the earlier stages under consideration the flat, two-dimensional surface was our sole area of interest. Notice in this stage that the integrity of the monolith is still maintained.
17A. Student Project: Concave-Convex Mass (pine).
17B. Nature: Female Torso.
17C. Man-Made Object: Terra Cotta Mexican Sculpture.

Step Eighteen: Space has entered the solid mass and pierced it; this penetration hints at the ultimate destruction of solid three-dimensional form.
18A. Student Project: Penetrated Mass (plaster).
18B. Nature: Driftwood.
18C. Man-Made Object: Hand Drill.

134

Step Nineteen: Three-dimensional mass is still dominant but a serious penetration by negative space has begun a significant alteration in the character of the positive mass. We notice particularly in the sculptural form of figure 19A that the surface of this form is taking on a plane-like or planar character. Such a surface will dominate the next few steps of this continuum.
19A. Student Project: Penetrated Mass with Developing Planar Surfaces (plaster).
19B. Nature: Crab Shell.
19C. Man-Made Object: Artist's Anatomical Figure.

Step Twenty: Here we observe the classic character of the fully planar form. It is still closed; by that we mean that the space which the plane describes is clearly delineated and no real penetration by the environment of space takes place into the planar forms.
20A. Student Project: Closed Planar Form (paper).
20B. Nature: Milkweed Pods.
20C. Man-Made Object: Gramophone, circa 1895.

Step Twenty-One: In this stage of the continuum, planar forms still describe space, but they are rapidly deteriorating and fragmenting into multiple and smaller surfaces. Space is still articulated by their surfaces but deep spatial intrusions imply the full dissolution of three-dimensional form into its last stage of line.
21A. Student Project: Evolving Planar Form (metal).
21B. Nature: Gladiola.
21C. Man-Made Object: Hotel Washstand, circa 1910.

135

Step Twenty-Two: Here we observe that planar forms which can be described as open for the intrusions of space are almost complete.
22A. Student Project: Open Planar Form (paper).
22B. Nature: Dried Seed Pod.
22C. Man-Made Object: Mexican Candelabra.

Step Twenty-Three: In this trio of forms, the planar form has sacrificed itself almost completely to the penetrations of an unrelenting spatial environment. Here the edges of the planar forms begin to etch and describe lines in this three-dimensional planar-linear composition.
23A. Student Project: Planar-Linear Form (glass).
23B. Nature: "Silver Dollar" Plant.
23C. Man-Made Object: Early American Spinning Wheel.

Step Twenty-Four: In this final phase of the design continuum only line remains to describe the character of the spatial environment. It might interest the reader to turn back to the first trio in this section: the two-dimensional linear composition of the first page can now be joined to the present three-dimensional phase and the figure, cycle, or field as the case may be, can be closed. In this manner, the entire continuum takes on its particular unity.
24A. Student Project: Three-dimensional Linear Form (balsa wood).
24B. Nature: Reeds.
24C. Man-Made Object: Bird Cage.

136

Glossary

Alla prima. An Italian term meaning "at one go." Denotes an oil painting technique in which a painting is completed in one operation from start to finish, wet-in-wet. Used to achieve spontaneity and freshness. Van Gogh was a master of alla prima.

Atmospheric spatial projection. In this projection method the illusion of space is accomplished mostly by diminishing detail as objects recede, retaining linear perspective through a kind of shorthand. Results are similar to the hazy effects observed on cloudy or misty days. Rubens, Watteau, Tiepolo, and Turner were masters of the technique.

Color-space projection. A broken-color technique that calls on the viewer's eye and mind to mix juxtaposed colors for the desired effect. The Impressionists, influenced by the French physicist Chevreul, developed a conscious school of such color-space manipulation. Georges Seurat's Pointillist experiments took the movement a step further; it became formalized in the work of Mondrian and Albers. The "Op" art movement is a direct outgrowth of these studies.

Concave-convex mass. A monolithic mass whose surface reveals depressions and projections.

Constructivism. Space structures created by utilizing planes and lines and emphasizing space rather than mass. This movement was begun in Russia about 1920.

Continuum. Any series of events that flow from one to another in an uninterrupted manner. A continuous whole, quantity, or series.

Cubism. [See Cubist spatial projection.] A radical art concept evolved by Picasso and Braque early in the 20th century to express the whole idea of an object by combining several views. Cubism is usually divided into two phases: analytical Cubism and synthetic Cubism. Analytical Cubism is an objective investigation of simultaneous images of an object, which are fractured into many cube-like planes. In synthetic cubism the object is redesigned and often simplified; bold, high chroma color is employed instead of the muted ochres and browns characteristic of analytical cubism.

Cubist spatial projection. This is the conscious effort of cubists to project spatial illusion off the surface toward the space of the observer. Together with the multi-faceted view on a two-dimensional surface, it represents one of the most original and significant innovations in the entire history of art. Although Cubism as a technique soon passed, it represents a major source for subsequent Abstract art forms.

Dematerialization. Physical and visual loss of mass.

Design continuum. A visual sequence conceived by the authors which describes the development of form from a two-dimensional plane through texture, relief, and environmental reliefs to monolithic mass and then proceeds to define its consequent dissolution by space into concave-convex, penetrated, planar, planar-linear, and three-dimensional linear forms. This visual sequence may be used to study the form of any type of object, natural or manmade.

Encaustic painting. A mixture of hot wax and pigments applied to a hard surface with heated spatulas or palette knives, and afterwards fused by passing hot irons over the painted surface. This is one of the oldest painting techniques known. It was employed by the Egyptians, Greeks, and Romans, and is still used by contemporary painters for its immediacy and rich textural quality.

Environment. That which surrounds or encompasses; may be either form or space or both.

Environmental relief. A relief that acts as an environment for subordinate three-dimensional forms emerging from its surface.

Environmental sculpture. A three-dimensional form that exists in a relief environment of equal emphasis.

Form. [1] The general visual appearance of an object or event. [2] Solid mass as opposed to space.

Found art. Objects whose form is not an intentional creation but which possess a notable esthetic worth.

Frame of reference. The psychological or physical position from which a person views a particular subject.

Futurism. A modern art form utilizing the essential elements of speed, power, and the machine for inspiration. Initiated in Italy early in the 20th century by the poet Filippo Tomasso Marinetti. The space-time paintings of Umberto Boccioni and Carlo Carra, early protagonists of this movement, anticipated the space-time motion picture image and the kinetic sculpture of Alexander Calder and Jean Tinguely.

Geometric projection. A method of projection that makes little or no attempt to create an illusion of space, being concerned mainly with clarity of symbolic expression. Word-picture languages such as the Egyptian hieroglyphics, Chinese and Japanese calligraphy, and American Indian symbols are the basis for many geometric forms of projection. Such forms tend to focus on scale in relationship to the importance of the object rather than spatial illusion.

Glazing. Transparent films of darker oil paint applied to lighter under layers, making possible an incredible luxury of detail. This was part of the early oil technique of Flanders [the Van Eyck school], later introduced into Italy. Glazing technique is still widely employed today.

Grid projection. A graphic technique in which the picture plane is divided into a grid that is used as a basis for establishing proportionate areas. This method is fully explained in Karl Gerstner's work *Designing Programs*.

Ground forms. A three-dimensional form seen in conjunction with a surrounding relief environment.

Illusory space. The illusion of three-dimensional space on a two-dimensional surface.

Impasto. A thick application of paint with sufficient body to retain the textural character of brushstroke or palette knife applications. Rembrandt mixed a small amount of wax with his oil pigments to give additional body to his rich impasto areas. Goya, Van Gogh and Courbet were masters of impasto technique.

Infinite space projection. This technique is used to imply infinite space extending beyond the boundaries of the picture. It is particularly notable in the Non-Objective school of painting, particularly the work of the Abstract Expressionists such as Pollack, Kline, Gorky, DeKooning, and Wassily Kandinsky. These painters increased the size of their canvasses to such dimensions that the spectator is literally engulfed by the painting.

Mobile. A three-dimensional form that incorporates movement in its design; also a specific genre of kinetic sculpture.

Monolithic mass. Absolute three-dimensional form, closed and resistant to the intrusion of space.

Motion picture projection. A profound art form that succeeds in transforming a two-dimensional plane [the screen] into a compelling illusion of three-dimensional space. One of the most, if not the most, significant spatial projection techniques of our time.

Negative space. The background or environment for a two-dimensional shape or three-dimensional form. Also called the ground area in the Gestalt figure-ground image.

Organic. Possessing the complex structure, rhythm, and interrelationships of a living thing (organism).

Parallel projection. A two-dimensional spatial projection technique in which lines that depict a plane receding into space remain parallel to each other, instead of converging as they do in perspective projection. Employed in Chinese and Japanese painting. In Japanese screen painting, parallel projection tends to maintain the screen surface as flat-decorative space.

Penetrated mass. A three-dimensional form fully penetrated by space, either by deep pockets or holes.

Perspective projection. [One, two, and three point.] A method of creating the illusion of a third dimension on a two-dimensional plane, invented by the Florentine architect Filippo Brunelleschi. This discovery transformed western art and dominated most western painters' conception of space from the 14th to the late 19th century.

Planar form. A three-dimensional form made up of plane-like surfaces which articulate space, permitting it to flow freely within the composition.

Planar-linear form. A three-dimensional form created by a combination of planes and lines in space.

Plane. A two-dimensional surface which may be either flat or curved.

Plastic spatial projection. This technique overlaps perspective projection but places its primary emphasis on the rendering of plastic form; all background detail is suppressed so that the illusion of the plastic form can be maximized. The method grew out of the greater understanding of light and plastic form achieved during the Italian Renaissance. The portrait heads of Antonello Da Messina are classics of this genre.

Positive space. A form or shape seen against a background which encompasses it, i.e., figure as opposed to ground.

Projection. An illusory extension beyond the normal surface of a two-dimensional plane, e.g., the picture plane. The illusion of spatial projection may attempt to project an image off the surface of the picture plane towards the spectator's eye, or it may attempt to project the spatial illusion into the surfaces of the picture plane. In some spatial projection techniques, no spatial illusion is attempted.

Relief. Ornamental projections that form an essentially two-dimensional plane. High, middle, low (bas) are used to describe the degree of projection. In design continuum terms: the in-and-out re-formation of the plane without destroying the continuity of its surface and the frontal aspect of a two-dimensional work.

Sculpture with base. A three-dimensional form with a subordinate base from which it emerges.

Shape. A two-dimensional area whose boundary may be defined by line or contrast in value, hue, chroma, or texture.

Space-time continuum. The "fourth dimension" which considers objects undergoing a transformation in both space and time as any moving object or motion picture.

Stabile. A three-dimensional form which is fixed in space.

Subjective spatial projection. This is a term used to described a new esthetic exploration of the human unconscious, based on the works of Freud, which opened a new world to the artist. Both the Expressionists and the Surrealists departed from traditional subject matter and techniques when they attempted to express emotional and subjective interpretations of man's inner life in terms of art.

Texture. A tactile quality produced by the juxtaposition of many relatively small three-dimensional elements on a surface.

Three-dimensional linear form. A three-dimensional form whose volume is described by lines in space.

Value. The degree of lightness or darkness relative to black or white.

Virtual volume. A volume defined by the path of a moving form in space or by the negative space enclosed within the boundaries of an object.

Bibliography

Compiled and annotated by Robert N. Fisher

In the process of researching the literature relating to this book, the authors discovered the need for a comprehensive bibliography in the fields of design and form and space. The resulting bibliography comprises over 150 works organized into the following categories: Design, Form in Nature, Form and Space, Graphics, Painting, Sculpture, Architecture, and Visual Arts: General. The annotations include comments concerning the relationship of the contents of the books to the theory of the Design Continuum, when applicable. It is hoped that the layman, student, and instructor will make ample use of the many excellent books that can provide other frames of reference for the study of form and design.

Design

Anderson, Donald, *Elements of Design.* New York: Holt, Rinehart and Winston, 1961.
A book dealing almost entirely with two-dimensional graphic representation, making little reference to three-dimensional form. It discusses in depth motivation, perception, sources (nature and man), line and tone, texture, symbol, point of view and movement, materials, expression in word form, color, and color symbolism.

Ballinger, Louise B., and Vroman, Thomas F., *Design: Sources and Resources.* New York: Reinhold Publishing Corporation, 1965.
A brief but convincing comparison of natural and man-made designs and forms, with interesting sections on nature, design principles, decoration, and contemporary design.

Bates, Kenneth F., *Basic Design: Principles and Practice.* Cleveland: World Publishing Company, 1960.
Of particular interest are Bates's chapters on spot, line, shape, and their grouping. Two-dimensionality is stressed.

Bayer, Herbert, and Gropius, Walter, *Bauhaus, 1919-1928.* Boston: Charles T. Branford Company, 1952.
The Bauhaus and its principles of design education are recorded in considerable detail.

Bel Geddes, Norman, *Horizons.* Boston: Little, Brown and Company, 1932.
The philosophy and experiments of this prolific visionary provide interesting commentary on the art of design and production for society.

Bevlin, Marjorie E. *Design Through Discovery.* New York: Holt, Rinehart and Winston, 1963.
A comprehensive survey of design in its many forms, with no new enlightenments but good general reference material.

Cannon, N. I., *Pattern and Design.* London: Lund, Humphries and Company, Ltd., 1948.
This somewhat oversimplified book is satisfactory for the junior or senior high school student.

Collier, Graham, *Form, Space and Vision.* Englewood Cliffs: Prentice-Hall, Inc., 1963.
This book stresses awareness and intuitive creative processes. There are good chapters on skeletal objects, planes, and surfaces in tension. The book contains detailed experiments that can be followed by the student.

Downer, Marion, *Discovering Design.* New York: Lothrop, Lee and Shepard Company, 1947.
A basic and simple book for the high school level. It discusses some principles of design seen in nature and man-made forms.

Emmerson, Sybil, *Design, a Creative Approach.* Pennsylvania: Laurel Publishers, 1953.
This general reference and "teach yourself" book has some highly interesting comments, but the illustrations and photographs, especially of student work, are of rather poor quality.

Farr, Michael, *Design in British Industry.* Cambridge: Cambridge University Press, 1955.
An extensive review of British industrial design until 1955, discussing data (materials), design organization, conclusions on the attitudes of industry toward the industrial designer, market research, and so forth, with suggestions for improvement in the field.

Felsted, Carol J., *Design Fundamentals,* third edition. New York: Pitman Publishing Corporation, 1962.
An extremely basic and undeniably clear "teach yourself" design book dealing with two-dimensional design.

Gloag, John, *Design in Modern Life.* London: Allen and Unwin, Ltd., 1934.
A slightly out-of-date but still valid collection of criticism of applied design—architecture, town planning, industrial design, and clothing by some of the foremost British designers of the day.

Graves, Maitland, *The Art of Color and Design.* London, New York: McGraw-Hill Book Company, Inc., 1941.
The "Compleat Book of Design"! Exhaustive and exhausting. All the key formulas, proportions, color keys, and chromatic relationships that will guarantee beautiful designs—if that were all there is to it.

Hatze, Gerd, *Idea 55, International Design Annual.* New York: George Wittenborn, Inc., 1955.
This is primarily an industrial design book with applications for all the materials illustrated, such as china and pottery, plastic, glass, wood, textiles, metal, and so forth. Comments on design by Raymond Loewy, Russel Wright, and Misha Black are included.

Hurwitz, Elizabeth A., *Design, A Search for Essentials.* Scranton: International Textbook Company, 1964.

Itten, Johannes, *The Art of Color,* translated by Ernst Van Haagen. New York: Reinhold Publishing Corporation, 1961.
A profusely illustrated book dealing with both the subjective and objective attributes of color, using examples both from classroom experiments and masterworks of art. Certainly one of the clearest accounts of color phenomena available.

Itten, Johannes, *Design and Form: The Basic Course at the Bauhaus,* translated by John Maass. New York: Reinhold Publishing Corporation, 1964.
Some interesting experiments are shown, but the greatest value of this book lies in learning what the Bauhaus taught. All student examples have explanatory notes.

Kahn, Ely J., *Design in Art and Industry.* New York: Charles Scribner's Sons, 1935.
This book is of value for its description of design and crafts in the Far East, Europe, and the United States, as well as for its discussion of museums and schools.

Kaufmann, Edgar, Jr., *What Is Modern Design?* New York: Museum of Modern Art, 1950.
A short, clear discussion of design in general, with a bibliography and out-of-date photographs.

Kepes, Gyorgy, *Language of Vision.* Chicago: Paul Theobald Publishers, 1944.
Now considered a classic in the field, this book provides the reader with a vocabulary of visual expression with which to discuss all fields of art. Although the book deals primarily with painting, photography, and advertising design, Kepes's terminology can readily be extended to cover the three-dimensional experiences of sculpture and architecture.

Kepes, Gyorgy, *Education of Vision.* New York: George Braziller, Inc., 1965.
A timely and excellently presented discussion of education for visual design encompassing trains of thought by educators and designers here and abroad.

Klee, Paul, *Pedagogical Sketchbook.* New York: Nierendorf Gallery, 1954.
"A basic plan for part of the theoretical instruction at the State Bauhaus in Weimar." See particularly sections on line, on which

Klee is certainly qualified to speak.

Lustig, Alvin, *Collected Writings.* New Haven: Holland R. Melson, Jr., 1958.
This short and perhaps too subjective book is valuable for gaining an insight into practical design problems through Lustig's notes on his personal experiences in the fields of architecture and graphics.

Marks, Robert, *The Dymaxion World of Buckminster Fuller.* New York: Reinhold Publishing Corporation, 1960.
A rather complete picture of the man and his work. Of particular interest is the background and development of his geodesic domes—their geometry and structural basis; studying them can give the layman a feeling for the structural properties of linear compositions in three dimensions.

Michigan University College of Architecture and Design; 11th Annual Conference, 1954, *Design and the American Consumer.* Ann Arbor: University of Michigan Press, 1955.
This book is a record of a series of addresses by industrial designers at the University of Michigan Design Conference in 1954. Topics discussed are: "Design and the American Consumer," "The Status of Consumer Research," "The Common Man and Grand Rapids," "The Potential in Design Research," and "The Unitized Kitchen."

Moholy-Nagy, Laszlo, *The New Vision,* translated by D. M. Hoffman. New York: G. P. Putnam's Sons, 1932.
A prophetic and profound work on Bauhaus training in materials, volume, sculpture, space, and architecture.

Moholy-Nagy, Laszlo, *Vision in Motion.* Chicago: Paul Theobald and Company, 1956.
The design world owes a great deal to Moholy-Nagy's writings. In this excellent book he reveals his ideas on photography, industrial design, architecture, painting, sculpture, contemporary art, life, his approach to organic design, and the integration of the arts as taught at the Institute of Design in Chicago.

Morton, Alastair, and others, *The Practice of Design.* London: Percy Lund, Humphries and Company, Ltd., 1946.
In this book the design process in crafts, industrial design, and architecture is described by a number of prominent designers. A good reference.

Nelson, George, *Problems of Design.* New York: Whitney Publications, 1957.
This book has a good layout and some humor but is heavy on words and light on illustrations. Topics discussed are problems of design, art, architecture, and home planning.

Newton, Norman, *An Approach to Design.* Cambridge: Addison Press, 1951.
A must for designers, architects, and artists, this book contains a series of excellent discussions on the best approach to applied design. It deals with structure, process, continuity, relationships, functions, psychological necessity, the relation to biology, and the view of total design with its relationship to its environment.

Nobbs, Percy Erskine, *Design: A Treatise on the Discovery of Form.* Toronto: Oxford Press, 1937.
This early work on principles of art and design on form, color, scale, proportion, ornament, function, planning, architecture, graphics, and sculpture is useful for general reference.

Pasadena Art Museum, *California Design.* Pasadena: Published annually.
A beautifully illustrated collection of the year's best designs from California, in furniture, fabrics, pottery, toys, lighting, and so forth.

Pye, David W., *The Nature of Design.* New York: Reinhold Publishing Corporation, 1964.

de Sausmarey, Maurice, *Basic Design: The Dynamics of Visual Form.* New York: Reinhold Publishing Corporation, 1964.
A short, well-illustrated paperback book discussing some of the principles of basic design.

Seigal, Curt, *Structure and Form.* Translated by Thomas Burton. New York: Reinhold Publishing Corporation, 1962.

Scott, Robert, *Design Fundamentals.* New York: McGraw-Hill Book Company, Inc., 1951.
The book is essentially good on two-dimensional design, with a short examination of three-dimensional design.

Smith, Janet K., *Design: An Introduction.* New York: Ziff-Davis Publishing Company, 1946.
Design elements are analyzed simply with reference to many different photographs. This book is useful for general reference and includes a good bibliography.

Smith, Janet K., *A Manual of Design.* New York: Reinhold Publishing Corporation, 1950.
The most valuable section of this book is contained in pages 18 through 21, where various properties of design are summarized in a compact list.

Tucker, Allen, *Design and the Idea.* New York: American Federation of Arts, 1939.
Approached from a painter's viewpoint, this early work on design has some interesting sections on the essentials of design, stressing mostly two-dimensional design.

Wallace, Percy J., *The Technique of Design.* London: Pitman Publishing Corporation, 1952.

Wedd, J. A. Dunkin, *Pattern and Texture: Source of Design.* New York: Studio Publications, 1956.
A short but interesting approach to pattern and texture. Illustrated.

Wolchonok, Louis, *The Art of Three Dimensional Design: How To Create Space Figures.* New York: Harper & Bros., 1959.
An excellent, well-illustrated work in which the author breaks sculpture into a great many elements such as prismatic, cylindric, conical, spherical, ribbon, plane, sheet linear, flowing surfaces. It is interesting that he discusses sculpture almost purely from the standpoint of its mass rather than from its form and space. Especially good for students beginning to have an understanding for sculpture.

Yale School of Design, *Portfolio of Student Work.* New York: George Wittenborn, Inc. 1955.
This book is very brief but it contains excellent sections on the design program at Yale. Graphic design, photography, painting and drawing, three-dimensional design, and architecture are all represented.

Form in Nature

Blossfeldt, Karl, *Art Forms in Nature.* New York: E. Weyhe, Inc., 1929.
A series of 96 photographs of plant forms that clearly demonstrate the manifold sculptural effects to be seen in nature—linear, planar monolithic, reliefs, and so forth.

Feininger, Andreas, *The Anatomy of Nature.* New York: Crown Publishers, 1956.
A fine book using striking photographs of nature with a scientific and yet poetic accompanying text to "document the unity of natural things, their interdependence and their similarity, to show the beauty of the living function of form."

Strache, Wolf, *Form and Patterns in Nature.* New York: Pantheon Books, Inc., 1956.
A handsome collection of Strache's photographs of nature's forms and patterns, including aerial, telescopic, and microscopic views, with an explanation of each photograph.

Form and Space

Alexander, Christopher, *Notes on the Synthesis of Form.* Cambridge: Harvard University Press, 1964.
A highly specialized mathematical approach to programming the process of design.

Berenson, Bernhard, *The Arch of Constantine: Or the Decline of Form.* New York: Macmillan Company, 1954.
This is the first of a proposed series of essays on the decline and rediscovery of form. Its relevance to the Design Continuum lies in the Introduction and Epilogue, where Berenson points out the usefulness of an evolution and dissolution process for study and in the field of art history.

Bill, Max, *Form.* Basel: K. Werner, 1952.
Profusely illustrated with comments on form in nature, sculpture, industrial design, crafts, and architecture, this book tries to suggest of what a beautiful form consists.

Birren, Faber, *Color, Form and Space.* New York: Reinhold Publishing Corporation, 1961.
The principles of Gestalt psychology and of color perception as applied to our sense of dimension and actual three-dimensional form are clearly discussed in this book.

Focillon, Henri, *The Life of Forms in Art,* second edition. New York: Wittenborn, Shultz, Inc., 1948.
A difficult but extremely valuable analysis of form interpreted by an art historian—yet the book does not deal with art history in the usual sense of the term. There are excellent points on form, form in space, form and matter, styles, and metamorphoses.

Greenough, Horatio, *Form and Function: Remarks on Art.* Berkeley: University of California Press, 1947.
A classic work on design in general with immediate application to architecture and industrial design.

Langer, Susanne, *Feeling and Form: A Theory of Art.* New York: Charles Scribner's Sons, 1953.
A valuable discussion of art theory. Chapters 5, "Virtual Space," and 6, "The Modes of Virtual Space," are of particular interest.

Le Corbusier, *The New World of Space.* New York: Harcourt, Brace and World, Inc., 1948.
A look at the works and ideas of Le Corbusier, with some relevant comments regarding space and the relationship of architecture, painting, and sculpture.

Maeterlinck, Maurice, *The Life of Space.* New York: Dodd, Mead and Company, 1925.
This book is for those readers who wish to explore more deeply the concept of space-time and the fourth dimension, as it evolved in part from Einstein's theory, and its influence on the Cubists and the Futurists.

Thompson, D'Arcy W., *On Growth and Form.* New York: Macmillan Company, 1948.
A monumental and fascinating approach to the relationship of growth and form and the role of physical forces on natural forms. Uses many mathematical models in its morphological study of organic form. For the advanced reader.

Trier, Eduard, *Form and Space: Sculpture of the Twentieth Century,* translated by C. Ligota. New York: Frederick Praeger, Inc., 1962.
Discusses contemporary sculpture from its expression of form and space.

Whyte, Lancelot, *Aspects of Form: A Symposium of Form in Nature and Art.* New York: Farrar, Straus & Giroux, Inc., 1951.
An important and comprehensive work in which the topic of form is approached by the

astronomer, scientist, biochemist, psychologist, biologist, physiologist, and artist. It creates an awareness of the depth and complexities of the physical and visual form.

Wolfflin, Heinrich, *The Sense of Form in Art.* New York: Chelsea Publishing Company, 1958.
A comparative study of German and Italian painting, sculpture, and architecture, with some interesting observations in Chapter I, "Form and Contour," and in Chapter VII, "The Relief Conception."

Graphics

Baker, Stephen, *Visual Persuasion.* New York: McGraw-Hill Book Company, Inc., 1961.
A penetrating visual and verbal analysis of graphic design, its appeal to the subconscious, and applications to contemporary advertising.

Ballinger, Raymond A., *Layout.* New York: Reinhold Publishing Corporation, 1956.
This book discusses a wide variety of problems associated with composing the two-dimensional surface to create a desired effect upon a viewer.

Baranski, Matthew, *Graphic Design: A Creative Approach.* Scranton: International Textbook Company, 1960.
This is a how-to-do-it book designed for high school students and their teachers. It explores many various techniques and materials on an elementary level.

Gerstner: Karl, *Designing Programmes.* Switzerland, Arthur Niggli, Ltd., 1964.
This fascinating and relevant book presents the concept of the programmed work of art— especially in the areas of graphics. Gerstner describes the graphic grid system, the morphological box, type face development, and two-dimensional art forms of an "Op-Art" variety.

Gerstner, Karl, and Kutter, Markus, *The New Graphic Art.* Switzerland: Arthur Niggli, Ltd., 1959.
An international pictorial survey of graphic art, from its origins through present-day achievements.

Lewis, John N., *Graphic Design.* London: Routledge and Kegan Paul, 1954.
This book traces the development of lettering, typography, and illustration up to the present, with emphasis on "the marriage of art to the technical process."

Rand, Paul, *Thoughts on Design.* New York: George Wittenborn, Inc., 1947.
A valuable book for the graphic designer. It "attempts to arrange in some logical order certain principles governing contemporary advertising design," such as symbol, humor, montage, collage, repetition of words or pictures to create texture, movement, rhythm, and typography.

Sutnar, Ladislav, *Visual Design in Action.* New York: Hastings House, 1961.
A prominent graphic designer and educator discusses his work and two-dimensional design in general. Profusely illustrated.

Painting

Albers, Josef, *Interaction of Color.* New Haven: Yale University Press, 1963.
A classic work on color, written by a leading exponent of psychological color phenomena. Albers directed the Yale School of Design for several years, during which time he influenced many of today's leading painters. His paintings demonstrate his theory of the interaction of color. The book is illustrated with original silk screen plates and is already a collector's item.

Berkman, Aaron, *Art and Space.* New York:

Social Sciences Publishers, 1949.
An excellent reference on the concept and development of space in painting, including Chinese, Byzantine, medieval, Renaissance, 16th- through 19th-century art, Cézanne, Cubism, and Abstract art.

Dember, William N., *The Psychology of Perception.* New York: Holt-Dryden, 1960.
Although this book is written for the psychology student, Chapter 5, "The Organization of Visual Perception," and Chapter 8, "Set and Perception," are clear and concise statements on what we see and why. An excellent book for the art student to own.

Evans, Ralph, *An Introduction to Color.* New York: Wiley and Sons, 1948.
An excellent overview of the physics of color and psychological color phenomena.

Gettens, Rutherford J., and Stout, George L., *Painting Materials.* New York: D. Van Nostrand Company, Inc., 1942.
This is an excellent book for the layman and student alike on the materials used in painting. It discusses mediums, adhesives, film substances, pigments, solvents, supports, tools, and equipment.

Gombrich, Ernst Hans Josef, *The Story of Art.* London: Phaidon Press, 1962.
A general survey of the history of art with good text and illustrations.

Gray, Christopher, *Cubist Aesthetic Theories.* Baltimore: Johns Hopkins Press, 1953.
An analysis of the three phases of Cubism, the refinement of early theories, and the development of aesthetic space-time relationships.

Hardy, Arthur Cobb, *The Handbook of Colorimetry.* Cambridge: Massachusetts Institute of Technology Press, 1936.

Hauser, Arnold, *The Social History of Art,* two volumes, translated in collaboration with the author by Stanley Godman. New York: Alfred A. Knopf, Inc., 1951.

Kandinsky, Wassily, *Concerning the Spiritual in Art, and Painting in Particular, 1912.* New York: Wittenborn, Wittenborn and Schultz, 1947.
Commentary on form and color, representation and abstraction, and their spiritual values and functions in relation to the observer and the artist.

Malraux, André, *Les Voix du Silence.* Paris: La Galerie de la Pléiade, 1951.
A classic discussion of style in all art forms. This work is available in translation. It is one of the finest works of critical thought in relationship to the arts in this century. A must for the student of art.

Mondrian, Piet, *Plastic Art and Pure Plastic Art.* Copyright: Harry Holtzman, 1945.
The artist discusses his thoughts on figurative and abstract art, the use of color and space, and the principles that guided his own painting.

Pope, Arthur, *An Introduction to the Language of Drawing and Painting,* Volume 1. Cambridge: Harvard University Press, 1939.
A valuable discussion of color theory. A theory of the growth and emergence of a defined form, space, and dimensionality in painting relates to the Design Continuum in approach.

Praeger, *The Praeger Picture Encyclopedia of Art.* New York: Frederick Praeger, Inc., 1958.
An excellent reference work in which a vast amount of material is readily available. Fine color and black and white plates.

Rasmussen, Henry M., *Art Structure.* New York: McGraw-Hill Book Company, Inc., 1950.
A detailed analysis of the structure of two-dimensional design which discusses tension, recession, depth, and so forth. Although there is little or nothing on three-dimensional design, this book is recommended for painting

analysis and for its bibliography.

Read, Herbert, *A Concise History of Modern Painting.* New York: Frederick Praeger, Inc., 1959.
An intelligent overview of modern painting with the usual Read insight and style.

Reward, John, *The History of Impressionism.* New York: The Museum of Modern Art, 1946.
One of the finest books in print on Impressionism.

Seitz, William C., *The Responsive Eye.* New York: Museum of Modern Art, 1965.
A well-illustrated, clearly written, concise presentation and summary of the background, premises, and main exponents of "Op-Art."

Taylor, Joshua C., *Futurism.* New York: Museum of Modern Art, 1961.
A thorough view of the "manifesti" and the development of the Futurists, with particular emphasis on Balla and Boccioni.

Sculpture

Adriani, Bruno, *Problems of the Sculptor.* New York: Mierendorf Gallery, 1943.
A general look at the concept of sculpture. See in particular Chapter 3, on relief, and Chapter 4, on sculpture in the round.

Appel, Karel, *The Sculpture of Karel Appel.* New York: Harry N. Abrams, Inc., 1963.
Appel's violent painted forms combine a gnarled sculpture with painting, creating violent distortions of the sculpture surface due to advancing and receding color and contrast relationships.

Archipenko, Alexander, *Archipenko: Fifty Creative Years, 1908-1958.* New York: Tekhne, 1960. Copyright, Mrs. Frances Archipenko.
A broad discussion on contemporary concepts of space by the sculptor, whose work in this area, whether philosophical or visual, has undoubtedly affected a great majority of today's sculptors.

Argen, Giulio C., *Pietro Consagra.* Neuchatel: Editions du Griffon, 1962.
The contemporary Italian sculptor has many works that exhibit the character of penetrated forms prior to open planar forms.

Barr, Margaret S., *Medardo Rosso.* New York: Museum of Modern Art, 1963.
An excellent reference examining problems that Rosso undertook to solve—especially the extension of the sculpture into the environment. He has a series of works that range from high relief to environmental forms, to sculpture with base, to full monolithic sculpture.

Eliosofon, Eliot, *The Sculpture of Africa.* New York: Frederick Praeger, Inc., 1958.
A magnificently illustrated book on African forms that have influenced much of modern sculpture. The full range of forms, from flat linear patterns to lines in space, may be seen.

Giedion-Welcker, Carola, *Constantin Brancusi.* New York: George Braziller, Inc., 1959.
Brancusi's forms can be seen to range from his famous monolithic sculptures, like *Birds* or *Torso of a Young Girl,* to the slightly more penetrated forms, as in *Mlle. Pogany* or *The Chief,* to strongly penetrated forms, as in *Socrates,* and finally to the almost planar forms in his Fish Series.

Giedion-Welcker, Carola, *Contemporary Sculpture, and Evolution in Volume and Space.* New York: George Wittenborn, Inc., 1955.
A profusely illustrated extension of an earlier work, including a superb bibliography. The concept of dematerialization of mass is discussed.

Giedion-Welcker, Carola, *Modern Plastic Art, Elements of Reality, Volume and Disintegration.* Zurich: H. Girsberger, 1937.
An excellent review of the evolution of modern sculpture to 1937, with many illustrations

and comments.

Gnudi, Cesare, *Mario Negri.* Milan: Edizioni del Milione, 1962.
Here we see Negri's work in various stages of penetrated forms, moving to planar forms, and some sculpture with base and environmental relief forms.

Marchiori, Guiseppe, *Luciano Minguzzi.* Milan: Edizioni del Milione, 1962.
Minguzzi's sculpture is primarily conceived of in planar, planar-linear, and linear forms, all of which are excellent examples of these areas of the Design Continuum.

Maryon, Herbert, *Modern Sculpture, Its Methods and Ideals.* London: Pitman Publishing Corporation, 1933.
Although this book does not deal with contemporary sculpture, Chapter XXXV, "Relief," is worth studying for its discussion on low relief, inclined planes, hollows, and bosses.

Meilach, Dona, and Ten Hoor, Elvie, *Collage and Found Art.* New York: Reinhold Publishing Corporation, 1964.
A rather informative book which discusses the properties and "how-to" of collage and found art, using many varied examples.

Ponente, Nello, *Mastroianni.* Rome: Modern Art Editions, 1963.
One of the foremost modern Italian sculptor's work is presented in this beautifully illustrated volume. Of particular interest in Mastroianni's expressive use of material, his painted reliefs, and sculpture.

Ramsden, E. H., *Twentieth Century Sculpture.* London: Pleiades Books, 1946. A concise and well-illustrated review of sculpture of the first half of the 20th century.

Ramsden, E. H., *Sculpture: Theme and Variations Towards a Contemporary Aesthetic.* London: Percy Lund, Humphries and Company, Ltd., 1953.
A clear and comprehensive development of sculptural values—social, philosophical, and aesthetic—from Egypt to 1953. This book contains valuable comments on contemporary sculpture in relation to past forms and several references to Moholy-Nagy's five stages of sculptural development.

Read, Herbert, *The Art of Sculpture.* New York: Bollinger Foundation, 1956.
An excellent work that should be fundamental to the study of sculpture.

Rodin, Auguste, *On Art and Artists,* translated by Mrs. R. Fedden. New York: Philosophical Library, 1957.
In general, Rodin's comments on realism, nature, movement, drawing and color, women, thought, mystery, and the Louvre are not applicable to the Design Continuum; however, the illustrations of Rodin's sculptures, which range from low reliefs to planar forms, are worth studying.

Seitz, William C., *The Art of Assemblage.* New York: Museum of Modern Art, 1961.
An excellent study of the development of assemblage, from Picasso and Braque. This book particularly applies to the Design Continuum in its discussion of the idea of illusion of space versus actuality and the thrust into space of elements in a painting.

Selz, Jean, *Modern Sculpture, Origins and Evolution,* translated by Annette Michelson. New York: George Braziller, Inc., 1963.
A beautifully illustrated book on exactly what its title states. It is a good general reference on sculpture.

Smith, David and Carandenti, Giovanni, *Voltrone.* New York: Harry N. Abrams, Inc., 1964.
The sculpture of David Smith should be studied for Smith's use of planes and lines in space in these works finished just prior to his death.

Soby, James, Editor, *Arp.* New York: Museum of Modern Art, 1958.
From an article "Arp—An appreciation" by Carola Giedion-Welcker, this is profusely illustrated work showing the broad spectrum of Arp's work, ranging from flat collages to textured surfaces of tar paper and glue, to low reliefs and ground forms, through monolithic and penetrated forms.

Sweeney, James J., *Henry Moore.* New York: Museum of Modern Art, 1946.
A visual and verbal summary of Moore's development in sculpture which is particularly useful in separating the ideas of "carving" and "modeling." It discusses the influences affecting the form of Moore's sculpture.

Sylvester, David (editor), *Henry Moore, Sculpture and Drawings. 1921-1948.* London: Percy Lund, Humphries and Company, Ltd., 1957.
A definitive work on Moore, leading to an excellent understanding of his background, sculpture, ideas on nature, drawing, use of organic forms, primitive art, and so on.

Valsecchi, Marco, *Umberto Milani.* Milan: Edizioni del Milione, 1962.
Milani's work ranges from painting to low relief through a series of exciting middle and high reliefs, monolithic form, through penetrated and, finally, open linear forms.

Werner, Alfred, *Modigliani the Sculptor.* New York: Arts, Inc., 1962.
The monolithic or slightly penetrated form of Modigliani's work is clearly in evidence in this book.

Wilenski, Reginald, *The Meaning of Modern Sculpture.* New York: Stokes, 1933.
A very good preparation for an understanding of contemporary sculptural values after 1933.

Architecture

Agard, Walter R., *The New Architectural Sculpture.* New York: Oxford University Press, 1935.
The relationship of sculpture to architecture is interestingly explored from a practical viewpoint. Sections on urban spaces, gardens, street furnishings, the pavement, stairs, water, trees, and movement. This is a revealing book that will greatly enrich the vocabulary of any reader.

Bitterman, Eleanor, *Art in Modern Architecture.* New York: Reinhold Publishing Corporation, 1952.
A valuable visual and verbal nontheoretical exploration of mainly contemporary and some historical uses of art in architecture. The techniques of canvas, fresco, fresco-secco, and mosaic murals and the use of stone, wood, metal, concrete, plaster, and ceramic for sculptural decorations are shown.

Bragdon, Claude, *The Frozen Fountain: Being Essays on Architecture and the Art of Design in Space.* New York: Alfred A. Knopf, Inc., 1932.
Bragdon is a proponent of organic architecture.

Breuer, Marcel, *Sun and Shadow.* New York: Dodd, Mead and Company, 1955.
The philosophy of this architect is interesting because it tends to conflict with Wright's concept of organic architecture; yet Breuer's houses still relate considerably to the landscape through his use of texture and materials.

Carver, Norman F., *Form and Space of Japanese Architecture.* Tokyo: Shokokusha, 1955.
A series of superb photographs of the forms and spaces in Japanese architecture, showing organic architecture, nature, and the house as an esthetic whole.

Conrads, Ulrich, *The Architecture of Fantasy,* translated by C. and G. Collins. New York: Frederick Praeger, Inc., 1962.
The proximity of sculpture to architecture is no better realized than in these works of fantasy and vision. When strict utilitarian concern is de-emphasized and the purely sculptural and/or spiritual aspects of the architecture are allowed to dominate, the result is one that resembles, in its philosophical and visual entirety, the work of a sculptor.

Damaz, Paul, *Art in European Architecture.* New York: Reinhold Publishing Corporation, 1956.
A superb book that stresses the synthesis of the arts resulting from their marked similarities of form and concept.

Fletcher, Donald A., *Introduction to Architectural Design.* New York: Mitre Press, 1947.
Although this book is composed as a series of step-by-step problems in architectural design, Fletcher's comments are very clear and useful, even to the nonarchitect who could familiarize himself with the issues of basic architectural design by examining the problems.

Gatz, Konrad, *Color in Architecture.* New York: Reinhold Publishing Corporation, 1961.
An excellent and persuasive work on the use and function of color in architecture.

Giedion, Siegfried, *Space, Time and Architecture.* Cambridge: Harvard University Press, 1954.
The classic reference work describing the development of modern architecture through a comparative historical analysis, examination of its relation to painting and sculpture, and, most important, through the refinement of and attitudes toward the concept of space.

Grillo, Paul J., *What Is Design?* Chicago: Paul Theobald & Company, 1960.
A chaotic but provocative book on various aspects of design, concentrating mainly on architecture. Grillo is admittedly dogmatic, but this sometimes makes for good reading.

Gris, Charles E. J., *Towards a New Architecture,* translated by Fred Etchells. London: Architectural Press, 1962.
Comments on form in architecture by one of the most influential architects of our time.

Gropius, Walter, and Tange, Kenzo, *Katsura: Tradition and Creation in Japanese Architecture.* New Haven: Yale University Press, 1960.
A discussion of the sculptural forms in the gardens and architecture of Japan's Katsura Palace, showing organic architecture and sculpture at its best.

Halprin, Lawrence, *Cities.* New York: Reinhold Publishing Corporation, 1963.
The city as a visual landscape is discussed in detail, with fine illustrations.

Hamlin, Talbot F., *Forms and Functions of Twentieth Century Architecture.* New York: Columbia University Press, 1952.
A four volume definitive analysis of the form and function of all major types of architecture in the 20th century.

Laurence, Frederick S., *Color in Architecture.* New York: National Terra Cotta Society, c. 1924.
An early work with some valid principles on the application of color to architecture.

Mumford, Lewis, *City Development: Studies in Disintegration and Renewal.* New York: Harcourt, Brace & World, Inc., 1945.
Mumford discusses the technical, sociological, and physical aspects of evolution and dissolution as applied to urban planning.

Muschenheim, William, *Elements of the Art of Architecture.* New York: Viking Press, Inc., 1962.
This excellent reference work provides an exceptionally clear analysis of the elements of form, surface, and space which compose architecture.

Peter, John, *Masters of Modern Architecture.* New York: George Braziller, Inc., 1958.
An excellent book in layout and use of photographs, which are profuse and well done. All

of the famous architects and then some are included in this reference work.

Ponti, Gio, *In Praise of Architecture*. New York: F. W. Dodge Corporation, 1960.
The famous Italian architect discusses his ideas on art, form, architecture, and a myriad of related subjects.

Rasmussen, Steen, *Experiencing Architecture*. Cambridge: Massachusetts Institute of Technology Press, 1962.
Highly recommended for the beginner as well as for the advanced student of architecture. A clear, unpretentious, and extremely revealing work on the most important principles of architectural design.

Rudofsky, Bernard, *Architecture Without Architects, An Introduction to Non-Pedigreed Architecture*. New York: Museum of Modern Art, 1964.
The rich and varied forms of indigenous architecture are worth the careful study of architect, painter, sculptor, or designer. Long discarded as being merely picturesque, these works are fresh, expressive, and exciting sources for the contemporary designer.

Scully, Vincent, *The Shingle Style: Architectural Theory and Design from Richardson to the Origins of Wright*. New Haven: Yale University Press, 1955.
Bibliography: pages 164-174.

Schoffer, Nicholas, *Space, Light, Time*, translated by Haakon Chevalier. Neuchatel: Editions du Griffon, 1963. American Distributor, New York: George Wittenborn, Inc.

Wright, Frank Lloyd, *The Natural House*. New York: Horizon Press, 1954.
The architect discusses his views on organic architecture, its environment, space, and relation of inside to outside in this excellent book.

Wright, Frank Lloyd, *On Architecture*. New York: Grosset & Dunlap, Inc., 1941.
A potpourri of Wright's comments, among which are a number relating to form and organic architecture.

Wright, Frank Lloyd, *An Organic Architecture*. London: Percy Lund, Humphries and Company, Ltd., 1939.
Commentary by Wright on the organic relationship between architecture and society and between architecture and its environment.

Zevi, Bruno, *Architecture as Space*. New York: Horizon Press, 1957.
An excellent and informative analysis of architecture in terms of its spatial qualities, the relation of interior to exterior, and the expressive form.

Zevi, Bruno, *Towards an Organic Architecture*. London: Faber and Faber Company, 1950.
A detailed and comprehensive study of the idea and development of organic architecture as seen in modern Europe and in the work of Frank Lloyd Wright.

Visual Arts: General

Arnheim, Rudolf, *Art and Visual Perception*. Berkeley and Los Angeles: University of California Press, 1960.
A book of fundamental and profound importance to the visual designer. Arnheim discusses in great detail the psychology of visual perception, how the mind perceives balance, shape, form, growth, space, light, color, movement, tension, and expression. Of extreme import to our readers are Chapters III and V, on form and space.

Baldinger, Wallace S., *The Visual Arts*. New York: Holt, Rinehart & Winston, Inc., 1960.
A comprehensive yet sufficiently detailed analysis of the total field of visual arts, including studies of industrial design, crafts, architecture, sculpture, photography, illustrating and print-making, and painting. Although no new theories are advanced concerning the relationships of these arts, it is a useful research tool.

Beam, Philip C., *The Language of Art*. New York: The Ronald Press Company, 1958.
A monumental but traditional book on all phases of art. Good for general reference.

Dewey, John, *Art as Experience*. New York: Minton, Balch, c. 1934.
Dewey's definitive presentation of the esthetic experience of art as being of the same constituency as the experience of life. Natural and man-made forms reflect one another because both derive their identity from the forces of life itself.

Eitner, Lorenz, *Introduction to Art*. Minneapolis: Burgess Publishing Company, 1961.
A guide to the study of art, with some good, clear points.

Fry, Roger E., *The Arts of Painting and Sculpture*. London: V. Gollancz, Ltd., 1932.
Although this book is not clearly related to the Design Continuum, some comments on painter's space, on pages 102-157, are relevant. Mainly art history and criticism.

Hildebrand, Adolph, *The Problem of Form in Painting and Sculpture*. New York: Stechert Haefner, Inc., 1932.
An early, important work with some particularly relevant chapters on relief and the visual perception of form.

Kepes, Gyorgy, *The New Landscape*. Chicago: Paul Theobald and Company, 1956.
Today the world of science and optics has extended man's vision incredibly. Kepes has illustrated this new landscape of vision in a manner that creates a feeling of a visual relationship between science and art. Rather than view the scientific field with fearful withdrawal, Kepes contends that the artist should begin to assess the extra-ordinary visual creations of science as a source for new directions in his work.

Kepes, Gyorgy (editor), *The Visual Arts Today*. Middletown, Conn.: Wesleyan University Press, 1960.
This book presents "an assessment of the visual arts today" by a number of well-known critics and practitioners. Included in it are discussions on the social, historical, psychological, and physical settings of today's art; goals and motivations of a number of artists; and a section on advertising art and motion pictures.

Lowry, Bates, *The Visual Experience: An Introduction to Art*. Englewood Cliffs: Prentice-Hall, Inc., 1961.
Approached from the point of view of the observer, the artist, and the critic, this book is an examination of the visual experience of seeing a work of art. It contains an especially good section on physical space (Chapter 13).

New York Graphic Society, *Man Through His Art*. Greenwich: New York Graphic Society, 1965.
A series that extracts a universal picture of man's social and cultural development from his artistic production.

Read, Herbert, *Art Now: An Introduction to the Theory of Painting and Sculpture*. London: Faber and Faber Company, 1933.
This is a short, snappy, and clear discussion in typical Read fashion of the theory of art, symbolism, expressionism, Cézanne, Cubism, and Surrealism.

Read, Herbert, *The Meaning of Art*. London: Pitman Publishing Corporation, 1951.
A classic analysis of art forms in general.

Rublowsky, John, *Pop Art*. New York: Basic Books, Inc., 1965.
A debatable but valuable attempt at clarifying the background and reasons for the rise of Pop Art as seen in the works of Lichtenstein, Oldenburg, Rosenquist, Warhol, and Wesselman.

Sewter, Albert, *A Lecture on the Relationship Between Painting and Architecture in Renaissance and Modern Times*. London: Tiranti, 1952.
A provocative and fresh investigation of the use of painting in architecture, showing how the relationship between each art form has alternated from a position of subordination; the relationship between illusory space and physical space.

Student Participants

Jean Abbott
Ingrid Adelhardt
Janice Alaimo
Judy Anderson
Lars Anderson
Ronald Andrews
Barbara Antovil
Leslie Arnold
Donald Bacorn
Marcia Bard
Carol Barnes
Anne Barr
Betty Beitscher
Cara Bersani
Patti Bertocci
David Beskid
Vaughn Bode
Olga Bodnar
Tamara Bogdanovich
Susan Bronstein
Ann Buescher
Sandra Bulbert
Bonnie Burger
Kathy Butts
Stephen Carver
Albert Casatelli
Fran Chamberlain
Robert Charron
Melissa Clark
Ann Crosse
Liz Crounse
Carolyn Crowl
James Crump
Ann Cummings
Andrea Davis
Carol Davison
Adrianne Dedek
Mickey Doran
Joseph Drury
Marianna Eckhardt
Tish Edson
Bruce Faber
Connie Fehling
Marsha Feigin
Karen Fellows
Becky Fender
Jo Ann Francis
Joyce Gardiner
Kathi Giberman
Martin Gieschen
John Goodel
Sandra Guzielek
Elizabeth Hacker
Torrey Hallock
Suzanne Hamilton
Stephanie Hedges
Sheryl Heinbach
John Hershey
Nancy Herson
Vicki Hessan
Jeffrey Higgenbottom
Betty Hilfman
Matthew Holynski
Anne Horowitz
Pat Howard
Marcia Hughes
Bruce Jennings
Carryl Johnson
Polly Johnson
Stephanie Johnson
Marcy Kaplan
Murial Kaplan
Sarah Kapp
Peter Karassik
Lee Karkruff
Ted Keller
Paul Kelly
Carol Ketchledge
Kelly Klose
Harry Kowadla
Sharon Kowal
Marie Krueger

Karen Kuracina
Peter Lee
Emily Leiding
Rosanna Licciardi
Carol Luder
Karen Lundquist
Judith Lupien
Cheryl Lutka
Joanne Lyman
Susan Mammosser
Celeste Manfredini
Emily Margles
Margaret Martin
Pamela Mason
Mary Matteson
Clare McBride
Hannah McLennan
Andrew McVicker
Susan Meyer
William Meyer
Joanne Miller
Marta Mitchell
Thomas Morin
Judith Nagler
Harold Nepo
Susan Newell
Judith Nightingale
Gene Orr
Joann Petta
Roberta Petteruti
Leslie Pitzer
John Powell
Helen Pozdniakoff
Alex Pregnar
Holly Putnam
John Reardon
Helen Reed
Nancy Reeves
Linda Roesch
Mary Roosa
Carlene Roters
Barbara Samuels
James Santiago
Ellen Scott
Martha Sears
Ellen Seigel
Diane Seltzer
Carolyn Shank
Marti Shohet
Adrienne Sholod
Ellen Siegel
Carol Silk
Patricia Sirhakis
Janice Slavis
Donna Spada
Sue Speak
Margaret Stires
Sandra Stockwell
Cheryl Streeter
Evelyn Sturgis
Patricia Susek
Richard Tanzmann
Paul Terpanjian
Marianne Thompson
Kathy Thornhill
Susan Tichenor
Nancy Tobin
Susan Travis
Kathy Vansteen
Couette Ventrone
Barbara Vogel
Carol Vollet
Laurie Walter
Cheryl Warren
Joan Weaver
Martha Weiss
Phyllis Whitcomb
Marsha White
Madelyn Wolff
Gail Yates
Jay Young
Phyllis Zent

List of Illustrations

Index

(Numbers in italics indicate illustrations.)